Meet to Marry

A Dating Revelation for the Marriage-Minded

By Bari Lyman

Health Communications, Inc.
Deerfield Beach, Florida

www.hcibooks.com

The names, locations, and other identifying information of the individuals in this book have been changed to protect their privacy. This book contains general information and is not intended to be, nor should it be, used as a substitute for specific psychological advice.

Library of Congress Cataloging-in-Publication Data

Lyman, Bari.
    Meet to marry : a dating revelation for the marriage-minded / Bari Lyman.
        p. cm.
    ISBN-13: 978-0-7573-1605-0 (trade paper)
    ISBN-10: 0-7573-1605-0 (trade paper)
    ISBN-13: 978-0-7573-9166-8 (e-book)
    ISBN-10: 0-7573-9166-4 (e-book)
    1. Dating (Social customs)   2. Mate selection.   3. Marriage.   I. Title.
    HQ801.L95 2011
    392.4--dc23

                                                                    2011031070

Publisher: Health Communications, Inc.
        3201 S.W. 15th Street
        Deerfield Beach, FL 33442–8190

Cover image © Getty Images/Image Source
Cover design by andCulture
Interior design and formatting by Lawna Patterson Oldfield

To Michael, my soul mate and partner in life.
Without you, it would not be possible

Contents

PART III ACT in the Present:
Dating for Marriage in Action

The Meet to Marry coaching program is made up of three parts: Assess, Attract, and Act to get you fully ready to begin dating for marriage and find the partner of your dreams. All of the forms you'll need are on the following pages in the book. In addition, all of these coaching materials are available at www.MeetToMarry.com.

Foreword

Love is a verb; it is an action that is the essence of all healthy relationships. I begin this foreword with a passionate statement about relationships, without which our existence as humans would be empty. We need one another to be. We need one another to become human. Emotionally fulfilling relationships are an integral component of mental and physical wellness. Our need to love and to be loved is universal. It is through this process that we can grow and become better partners. In our quest to connect with others on an intimate level, we must begin with unconditional love of the self and believe that we are lovable, based purely on our basic nature as humans. When we embrace full self-acceptance we can unconditionally love ourselves and others. We are born with a core self that need not be validated by others, but only by ourselves. Our psychological struggles are created by the interchange of our genetics and the environment. We have interjected our parent's deficiencies (their internalized past) and cultural conditioning. We operate on unconscious levels in most aspects of our lives, seldom questioning our beliefs, attitudes, or behaviors. We accept our thoughts and feelings as the Truth and insist that the environment should comply. We insist on being right rather than doing the right thing. This is especially true when it comes to our intimate relationships.

Therefore, finding the "right one" is accomplished by becoming the "right one." It is our internal journeys through which we discover our true character. Healthy encounters depend on the ability of each individual to be fully accountable for his/her thinking, feeling, acting, and relating. The level of personal maturity of each individual is highly correlated with the potential success of the relationship and its level of functioning. It is the man/woman in the mirror who has to be seen very clearly, or we will deflect our fears onto others. It is through the constant polishing of our own mirror that we become visible to ourselves, thus seeing the other for who they are without any judgment. It is only then that rational choices can be made, whether you are matched or not. Our relationships with our partners facilitate our growth and allow us to reach our potential. Each individual must value himself/herself in order to be committed to the work of building a partnership that moves from romantic love to a true attachment.

All beginnings are wonderful. Marriage is a serious commitment. This is where the level of personal maturity comes into play. It is the individual's capacity to move away from the Hollywood notion of love and get involved in the lifelong building of intimacy that will bring about true attachment. Marriage is for the tenacious, not for the weak. Marriage is a social, psychological, emotional, sexual, and economical "body" that needs to be nurtured and cared for on a daily basis. It is a system that has its own dynamics. It is the individual's capacity to choose the path of marriage when confronted with life's events, to surrender to the partnership and close all exits. It is the individual's courage to look at himself/herself when confronted with conflict, because there is a high probability that both are contributing to the problem. Solution-oriented couples are more functional. They spend most of the time negotiating solutions rather than engaging in criticism and blame.

It is important to remember that all of us have been conditioned by our culture. We have been told what to think, how to feel, how to behave, and so on. We become addicted to our thoughts, feelings, and actions. We accept all of it without questioning its truth. These attachments are the source of our psychological suffering. Our fear of being alone overrides our intuition when we encounter relationships that we know are not right for us. We convince ourselves that he/she will change, that he/she is having a bad day. In short, we are in the story. We are within our addictions. We are within our fears. We are not our best friends. We are not connected to ourselves. We are looking to be saved. We are regressing to being children. We are looking for our mothers/fathers. We are choosing not to parent ourselves. We are within our obsessive attachments. We are afraid to be free. We are afraid to grow.

We need to drop our conditioned belief that our happiness comes from attachments. True love is our ability to see others and ourselves without judgment. True love has no expectations or boundaries. A loving relationship is defined by living in harmony with ourselves while being visible to our partners. Our differences should not divide us but rather connect us. Our ability to assume responsibility for our actions is the bedrock upon which intimate relationships rest. Intimate connection is our map to a meaningful life. It is a human encounter of the best kind.

Meet to Marry is a passionate product of Bari's triumph and a testimony to the human spirit and our resiliency as a species. She has taken her life experience and transformed herself, dedicating her work to changing the lives of others. We must believe and trust that our spirit can transcend our wounds and move us toward our untapped and abundant potential. We must give our life meaning, as Bari has done by writing her book and creating the Meet to Marry program.

Remember, like life itself, nothing prepares us for marriage but marriage itself. It is a leap of faith in ourselves, and when we lose our way, mindfulness is the light that shows us the way back. Marriage is not the destiny of our quest, but rather the journey itself. It is the context within which two souls connect and grow through lifelong vulnerability to each other. It is the ultimate path to discover the wonders of human attachment.

Eli Levy, Ph.D.
Miami, Florida
March 2, 2010

Preface

I wrote this book as a celebration of what is possible for a human being. As the first Meet to Marry success story more than eight years ago, I wish to share a real message of triumph and hope for all single people who would like to find a partner with whom to live an exceptional life. Before Meet to Marry, my future was predictable: to be alone or in a continued pattern of unsatisfying relationships. I spent my life looking for love—but with all the wrong people. Though I was an educated, resourceful, good person, I was unequipped to know not only what I needed in love but also how to find it. So, for many years I continued to find myself wondering why love was so unsatisfying, why dating was a chemical experience, and why the people who I attracted not only didn't share my vision or values but—even worse—they saw my best qualities as liabilities.

Meeting men was not a problem—I could meet and attract them. The problem was finding appropriate men who could meet my unique needs to feel cherished and to share meaningful communication and partnership. These were concepts that, back then, meant nothing to me so they went unarticulated. Dating was an unconscious, primal search to not be alone. A former relationship disaster, as I lovingly call myself in retrospect, I twisted myself into various shapes and sizes in order to find ways to receive love from men who were ill suited for the job. My relationship history reflected how I felt about myself from my childhood: that "something is wrong."

Although I'd been doing personal development, self-help, and transformation work for more than twenty years, being in a healthy relationship was like an unsolved mystery. I'd always been successful in business, but never in finding and keeping the kind of love that I truly wanted.

There came a point in my life when I hit bottom, so to speak, and I questioned this painful, unending pattern of feeling alone, wishing people were different, trying to change them, trying to change myself . . . and to understand why, if I was a smart, attractive, successful, serial optimist with a lot of love to give, things just couldn't fall into place for me. But as I learned, things don't "just" happen. In order to have the kind of passionate and meaningful life I'd only imagined, something needed to change. As I discovered later, that change had to begin with me.

If *you* desire a loving relationship, a relationship designed to last a lifetime, it needs to *begin with you*, too. It is not only possible to attract the kind of person you want and desire, but it is 100 percent attainable. It will take an open mind, a new, refreshing, principled approach, and a simple paradigm shift.

This is the philosophy and the mantra of this book: to find *the one,* you need to *be* the one. That is what this book is about. It is this message of great hope and transformation that gives my life meaning, and I want to share it with you.

It was this realization—that I was in charge of my thoughts and that I could create my own reality—that was to become the next phase of my continued lifetime journey of personal change. This ultimately led me to meeting and marrying my divine husband, Michael, with whom, I am grateful to say, I live my dream life.

We are often seduced into believing the bankrupt messages we receive from society and the media, and we believe that our feelings are true, when in fact our feelings are just that—feelings. As you will read in the pages that follow, feelings are formed by the "meaning" we apply to the events in our lives and are not necessarily "the truth." While you may gather evidence that there is no one worth dating, and that the singles events are lousy, through reading *Meet to Marry*, you will see how your thoughts actually create your reality, and, more than likely, you will have a breakthrough in creating a new reality for yourself.

When I was attracting these mismatched men (narcissists, spiritually dissimilar, emotionally unavailable), it was actually *me* attracting them, creating what I unconsciously felt I deserved in a self-perpetuating, vicious cycle. While the evidence was mounting that the reasons were outside of myself ("they" were the problem), this was not the truth.

There are countless books and talk shows with expert guests bombarding you with information about how to externally fix yourself and change yourself to be better and more attractive to the opposite sex. However, if you have unrealistic expectations like *I must meet someone supermodel gorgeous/handsome* or you have a story inside of you (like I did) that tells you something is wrong with you or you don't deserve a healthy, happy relationship, then trying to break the pattern externally would be like putting a Band-aid on the problem. It's better to address the real issues of what is keeping you from love.

So, at the age of thirty-five, however well-intentioned I was, and regardless of how much I hoped that things would just "turn out"—that a great guy would magically appear in the distance to save me, one who would "get" me—I realized that he just wasn't coming. And so my journey began . . . and not a minute too soon.

It's on this foundation, one of clarity and principles, that *Meet to Marry* is based. As a former dating disaster who was able to turn it around and meet the greatest guy in the world—my husband, Michael, who cherished me from the moment we met—I am eternally grateful. I have dedicated my life to helping singles achieve the life they dream of, and it's what I wish for you.

The singles I coach and with whom I share this work experience a major shift in their dating and life experience, just as I did. At first they report developing an increasingly clear vision for themselves, and they are soon shocked at how the universal attraction principles kick in, with people and circumstances suddenly aligning with their vision. With a true desire for change and the willingness to commit to a different way of thinking, virtually anyone can meet their dream spouse now. Here, then, is the step-by-step process you'll use to find your ideal spouse (and yourself along the way).

1. *ASSESS* your marriage readiness.
2. *ATTRACT* the kind of person you desire.
3. *ACT* in the present to change your future.

These three steps will help you find yourself and your mate, and are designed to help you have breakthroughs as you proceed through this self-paced program. You'll find exercises, case studies, and support throughout. The Meet to Marry program is designed to enable you to experience a living and breathing opportunity for life-changing transformation. So sit back and relax while I share with you the methods and steps that will open the floodgates of joy to you, and a renewed commitment to having a loving, fulfilling marriage in your life.

How to Use This Book

This book is designed to guide you in achieving breakthroughs in your life. It's not designed for insights and intellectual conversations; it's a guide book for you to achieve real results. The most effective way to achieve breakthroughs from *Meet to Marry* is to use the tools of the coaching in your daily life. I recommend following the Assess, Attract, Act program in order, as each section builds on the previous one.

As in life, everything doesn't need to be perfect to produce actionable results. And since personal growth is not linear, feel free to use any of the tools in the Assess, Attract, or Act sections at any time. Within each chapter you'll find an exercise called "Have a Breakthrough" and a special Date to Marry Tip to support you on your journey.

At the end of the book, you'll find information about all of the coaching materials available at the Meet to Marry website. Whether you learn by seeing or by doing, you can take advantage of the entire coaching experience at www.MeetToMarry. com, where you'll find coaching courses, podcasts, programs, webinars, and more.

> *There's an expression that goes, "Even Michael Jordan has a coach." The greatest basketball player in the world needed support to reach and maintain his potential. You too can take advantage of the coaching approach to this book.*

The first part of the book, "ASSESS Your Readiness: Create Your Dating Revelation," explores the philosophy behind the need for a modern dating revelation and how the media, pop culture, and even dating coaches' well-intended messages are keeping you from love. We will explore how the rules of dating have changed in our modern world, deconstruct media and cultural stereotypes about relationships, and see how our own experiences have shaped our ideas about dating and marriage. The second part, "ATTRACT Your Ideal Spouse: Principle-Based Dating," explains how to become clear about your needs, how to date in this new way, and how to identify if someone is right for you. Part III, "ACT in the Present: Dating for Marriage in Action," includes Date to Marry Tips and positive, proactive actions to take while dating for marriage, and being the best you can be. You'll also read real-life success stories of couples who dated for marriage, their amazing experiences, and how it can work for you!

If someone like me could turn it around to find her dream husband and become a coach on the subject of dating for marriage, it can be simple for you, too. Simple, yes, but it will require commitment, an open mind, and earnest application of the tools and concepts that I'll share with you in the upcoming chapters.

Why I Created *Meet to Marry*

As a personal development champion who loves possibility, I have been involved in giving and receiving coaching, and matching people for more than twenty years. A graduate of Landmark Education, I'm a strong advocate for transformation and possibility, and I love to help people transcend their situations (much like I did).

I've taken my twenty-plus years of combined experience as a coach and mentor, my life experience of personal change, and intense study of dating and relationship strategies to develop the Meet to Marry coaching program and philosophy. In order to create the most effective, success-oriented "dating for marriage" program, I combined my personal insights and breakthroughs with the enduring principles from experts and mentors I highly respect, including Landmark Education, Steven Covey (author of *The 7 Habits of Highly Effective People*), Imago principles from Hartville Hendrix's *Getting the Love You Want* and *Keeping the Love You Find,* Hedy and Yumi Schleifer, Eli Levy, Ph.D., and others you will read about in the pages that follow. It is this mission of helping others get the love they want that gives my life meaning.

Through the process of my personal transformation, I kept a journal documenting the insights and the miraculous breakthroughs I had that finally caused me to change. All of this wisdom, combined with more than 10,000 hours' worth[1] of personal development and twenty-plus years of coaching, enabled me to shape the philosophy and program that I share with you.

The good news is that if you want to "find the one" and get married and it hasn't happened yet, 10,000 hours of personal development and coaching aren't necessary to get there. As you'll discover in the following pages, it simply requires uncovering blind spots that keep you from your happiness, taking on a positive mind-set, developing a clear vision and game plan, and committing to taking consistent steps toward putting that game plan into action and realizing that vision.

Having faith doesn't hurt either.

---

1 In his best-selling book *Outliers,* Malcolm Gladwell repeatedly mentions the "10,000-Hour Rule," claiming that the key to success in many fields is, to a large extent, a matter of exhaustive practice; that is, practicing a specific task for a total of at least 10,000 hours.

Part I

ASSESS
Your Readiness:
Create Your
Dating Revelation

**Every generation needs
a new revolution.**

—*Thomas Jefferson*

The Meet To Marry Coaching Program

The program is comprised of three parts: Assess—Attract—Act to get you "being" the one and fully ready and engaged in dating for marriage.

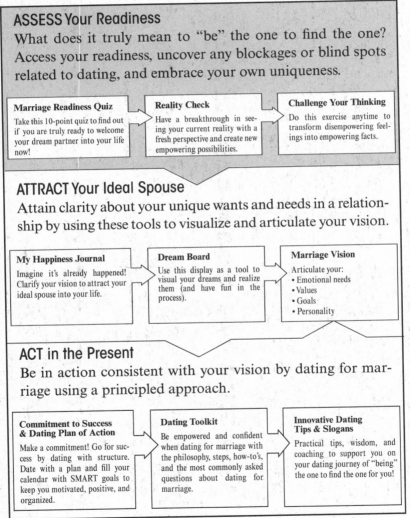

ASSESS Your Readiness
What does it truly mean to "be" the one to find the one? Access your readiness, uncover any blockages or blind spots related to dating, and embrace your own uniqueness.

Marriage Readiness Quiz
Take this 10-point quiz to find out if you are truly ready to welcome your dream partner into your life now!

Reality Check
Have a breakthrough in seeing your current reality with a fresh perspective and create new empowering possibilities.

Challenge Your Thinking
Do this exercise anytime to transform disempowering feelings into empowering facts.

ATTRACT Your Ideal Spouse
Attain clarity about your unique wants and needs in a relationship by using these tools to visualize and articulate your vision.

My Happiness Journal
Imagine it's already happened! Clarify your vision to attract your ideal spouse into your life.

Dream Board
Use this display as a tool to visual your dreams and realize them (and have fun in the process).

Marriage Vision
Articulate your:
• Emotional needs
• Values
• Goals
• Personality

ACT in the Present
Be in action consistent with your vision by dating for marriage using a principled approach.

Commitment to Success & Dating Plan of Action
Make a commitment! Go for success by dating with structure. Date with a plan and fill your calendar with SMART goals to keep you motivated, positive, and organized.

Dating Toolkit
Be empowered and confident when dating for marriage with the philosophy, steps, how-to's, and the most commonly asked questions about dating for marriage.

Innovative Dating Tips & Slogans
Practical tips, wisdom, and coaching to support you on your dating journey of "being" the one to find the one for you!

1

The Rules of Dating Have Changed

There are more than 100 million singles in America alone according to the U.S. Census Bureau; that's 40 percent of Americans. With statistics like that, and a trend toward living together rather than getting married, our society is demonstrating an aversion to, or a fear of, that which we were built for: deep and meaningful committed relationships.

We are all connected: our society, our planet, and all of humanity. We share our visions and values through relationships. We were born to connect and relate to each other and to be acknowledged. As human beings, we crave meaning in our lives.

Most of us will, at some point, ask the ever-important question, "Why am I here?" and we will look to our relationships, at least in part, for answers.

Fifty years ago, before the explosion of pop culture and technology, there would be no need for this book. When people dated in generations past, they dated to marry, and the approach they took to find potential matches was quite unlike today. Most people married young and dated within their communities, within their culture, and within their houses of worship or their clubs, and the expectation was that they were looking for a good husband or wife with whom they could build a family and a life.

They shared values because they were from the same tribes. They shared similar ideals, perspectives, and worldviews—there was commonality. Technology and a "flat world" have given us more choices of people to meet, but unfortunately, many of them will not share our values or ideals because they grew up in different cultures or with different value systems. More choices can be great, but only if you know what to look for.

Today, we live in a society where ideals and values have changed, and many of our role models are not great teachers or leaders with strong morals and values. More often, it's the rich and famous, rock stars, models, and sports figures we idealize. We are bombarded with superficial messages from the media and our culture that sex, good looks, and money are the ultimate ideals to strive for, and gender stereotypes are alive and well. The not-so-subtle message you receive about relationships is that they are disposable, and we all pay a big price for that thinking.

Why Should We All Be Concerned?

With 40 percent of Americans single and a divorce rate of 50 percent among first marriages and 60 percent among second and third marriages, our society is experiencing a real breakdown. Divorce is brutal and it affects our entire society—especially kids. As a child of divorce, I can tell you that stability begins at home with loving, mature parents who provide strong examples and an environment where kids can experience stability and emotional safety and develop healthy self-esteem. Functional, happy, healthy families can only be built through authentic relationships built on a solid foundation.

As we'll discuss in the upcoming chapters, a strong foundation begins with being a marriage-ready, mature person and then choosing a spouse you can be devoted to for a lifetime, through the good times and difficult times, especially those times when you need to be giving, understanding, and compassionate, and to close all exits when you feel like running the other way. (It's typical that when we leave an "unworkable" marriage, we usually find the same "unworkability" in the next marriage; only the partner is different.) By being marriage-ready and identifying a marriage-ready spouse, a marriage partner who shares your values, your vision, and your life goals—rather than buying into the disposable, superficial notion of marriage—we can all come to know a clear path to an enduring marriage.

So, in our society, where divorce is so prevalent, it's no wonder that many kids grow up to be confused and blocked in the relationship arena. Another way to go, a principled option, is to see marriage as a sacred bond worthy of commitment, introspection, and appreciation rather than the easy-come, easy-go, easy out.[2] At the heart of it, we all desire a meaningful connection, and that connection is found in relationships. As a society, we need to reinvent what is really important to us and what gives our lives true meaning. Most of us will define our successes by the lifetime of simple moments and important memories we shared with people we love and the difference we made with them.

Changing the Way We Think About Dating and Marriage

The Meet to Marry philosophy is a paradigm shift of principled, refreshing ways to think about marriage—and it's a philosophy that challenges the status quo. Imagine approaching every date as a fantastic exploration: no games, just authentic conversations with potential life partners. When dating for marriage, you discuss ideals, goals, and values up front; you do not choose a marriage partner based on interests, attraction, or media-inspired romance and fantasy.

When dating for marriage, you don't look for "love at first sight" because real, meaningful love grows and deepens from life experiences. When seeking lasting, meaningful love, you'll learn how to

---

[2] I am not advocating marriage as the answer for everyone or indicating that divorce is wrong. There are obviously many situations where divorce is the appropriate and healthy choice. Given a choice between being healthy and divorced or enduring intolerable situations, divorce is obviously preferable. However, in our society there is an overemphasis on divorce, and this is what I am addressing.

identify the characteristics to match someone perfectly for you in order to create a lifetime partnership. We all know happily married couples who say that they love their spouse more today than when they met, and that is the success I wish for you.

Many will consider what I propose in this book as radical. Radical, because the norm is to subscribe to mystery dating, where you feel compelled to hide the real part of "who you are" and wait until an unknown "right time" to discuss the important issues. A common question asked by singles is "How long should I wait to bring up the question of marriage with the person I am dating?"

Have you ever dated someone and didn't really know the other person's intentions—after three months, six months, or even multiple years? In the pages that follow, I will arm you with information, tools, and a rationale to eliminate mystery dating once and for all, and provide you with key principles so you can be marriage ready.

The wedding is just the beginning of the journey. In the movies, the dramatic last scene is always the wedding; the beautiful young couple kiss and then, "The End." But that's backward. In real life, true love begins *after* the wedding. Real love grows as your appreciation for your partner grows through life's experiences, empathy, and bonding. Real love is the appreciation of someone's goodness, inner beauty, character, and commitment, and this bonding comes with time, through meaningful attachment, and experience together.

A friend of mine was sitting with his father and said to him, "Dad, after five years of marriage, I think I finally understand what love is." The father said, "Wait till you're married twenty-five years, then you'll understand what love is." The grandfather was also in the room and overheard this exchange. He told them, "Wait till you're married fifty years. Then you'll really *understand what love is."[3]*

Creating a Powerful Marriage

This journey begins when you are open and happy with yourself, embracing your own uniqueness, clear about the kind of person you are looking for, and positive and excited about the adventure and possibilities open to you in searching for someone to share your life with.

This book is about finding someone with whom you can create a love affair and partnership that will last a lifetime. We'll discuss the elements involved in creating a marriage where love deepens over time through bonding, attachment, and life building. We'll discuss how you can attract your ideal spouse.

Attraction is important in finding your match, and yes, passion and intimacy are necessary elements in a marriage. However, lust is chemical. Lust and obsession are not enduring. The object of your love may be beautiful and handsome, and perhaps you can't stop thinking about him or her, but chances are this is infatuation. What happens when the infatuation wears off?

---

3 Rabbi Dan Silverman, "Three Ingredients of a Successful Marriage." http://www.aish.com/flm/19891477.html.

The Steps of the Meet to Marry Program

In this section, I'll discuss the overall structure of the program and the coaching philosophy. There are no quick fixes here, but a methodology and a path to follow if you want to find true love. The main principle upon which this program is based is the following:

To find The One, you need to Be The One.

The paradigm shift that is different from what everyone else is telling you is this: *You* will take personal responsibility for who you are "being" and who shows up in your life. *You* will become "the cause" of your life in the first step of the program, which is called "ASSESS."

1. Become your own best friend and advocate.

First, you'll connect to yourself and uncover blockages and blind spots that may be keeping you from your happiness. If you've been dating for a while, this may be just what you've been looking for. *You may not be aware that what you are thinking (even unconsciously) may be keeping you from your dream life.*

The intention is to have a breakthrough in your relationship with yourself and in how you view dating and marriage . . . *forever*. You'll get to see how your blockages, blind spots, and "stories" may be keeping you single, even if you aren't aware of them. (This is typically a mind-blowing exercise in personal transformation.) You'll learn how to become your own best friend and advocate with a new fresh attitude for dating and finding "the one." The tools you'll use to assess and uncover your blind spots include:

✓ Marriage Readiness Quiz page 28
✓ Reality Check page 74
✓ Challenge Your Thinking page 108

2. You'll become clear about yourself and the kind of person you want and need in a relationship.

In Part II of the book, you'll create a clear mental image of your future life and your ideal spouse (a tactile and powerful experience using your imagination and creativity). You'll create a picture of the kind of person you need in a relationship. Getting clear on who you are and the kind of person you need is very powerful and comes from your own inner essence. It's fun and magical to gain clarity about your own needs and use universal attraction principles (God, the universe, faith, Higher Power, etc.) to draw him/her into your life. You'll do this with the following tools:

✓ My Happiness & Finding My Life Partner Journal
✓ Meet to Marry Dream Board

Use the journal to stimulate your right brain to envision not only the practical elements of the life you'd like to create but the emotional ones as well. The questions in the journal will evoke answers from your imagination and your deepest desires. They relate not only to practical considerations of the kind of life you'd like to build, but emotional issues relating to how you'd like to feel in a relationship, how you and your partner will communicate, play together, and what it feels like to be with someone you love and who loves you unconditionally. The journal exercise, done in combination with the meditation and the dream board exercises, is a creative experience that will leave you with such clarity that when someone or something "other" than your vision shows up, you'll know instantly.

Next, you'll create your Marriage Vision by defining your unique personality and emotional needs and articulating your values and life goals. Your Marriage Vision is a compilation of you! You'll create a full picture of what makes you *you* by identifying what's really important to you in the areas that matter most. This takes the mystery and confusion out of figuring out what you really need for long-term happiness and satisfaction. You'll create your Marriage Vision and get in touch with the kind of person you truly want (and need) by:

- Expressing your *personality.*
- Evaluating your *emotional needs.*
- Identifying your *values.*
- Articulating your *goals.*

You can't search for a spouse if you don't know what kind of person will be right for you and what you truly and authentically desire. Let's take a closer look at these four areas:

Personality: As you'll read in more detail in Chapter 7, one of the top ways to choose a spouse is to find someone whose personality you love, someone to admire, someone with whom you will bond and share your life. In this exercise, you'll articulate your own personality and how and why you chose these personality traits; you'll express to others how your personality shines. For example, if you choose "kind" as one of your personality traits, you'll articulate why. Do you do charity work, volunteer with children, feel sensitive to the needs of others, and try to walk in other people's shoes? By thinking in depth about the various shades of your personality, you can articulate your personality to others and learn a few things about yourself along the way.

Emotional needs are needs that make you happy when met; when they are not met, it brings you right back to childhood (i.e., feeling and acting as you did when you were a child). And childhood is the place to look when identifying your emotional needs. We'll delve into this deeper, but to begin, here is an example of how critical it is to know your own emotional needs. My top emotional need is to be cherished. I was born into a situation where my needs were not met. So regardless of how much work I've done on myself and my level of personal transformation, I will always want and need to be cherished. In my life before my husband, Michael, my emotional needs went unarticulated, and I would twist myself into a pretzel, trying to fix myself in order to feel appreciated or cherished by the people I chose (or who chose me). In my new life, I wanted to attract and identify a husband who had the capacity to be "cherishing." Another important element in choosing a spouse is to find someone with whom you feel an emotional connection and bond, and a good place to start is by articulating your emotional needs.

Values are elements about yourself and another person that are very important to you. They relate to family, religion, finances, contribution, volunteerism, education, and more. They also relate to your principles, purpose, and life mission, and to personal qualities like honesty, integrity, loyalty, and generosity. By articulating what's important to you, you can remain true to your principles.

Here's how it works: You may be someone who values family. You may be clear about the fact that your marriage vision is to live in France and have many children. You may also value religion and education. You envision a life of adventure and you believe that life doesn't begin at sixty-five. In this example you prefer a life of experiences over acquiring and having "stuff" (financial values). These are some of your core values and part of your marriage vision. If you meet someone who doesn't have marriage on his or her radar, doesn't want to travel, is not into religion, and believes in saving all of his/her money for retirement, it certainly wouldn't be a great match.

If you meet someone and only discuss that you both love going to the movies and eating sushi and drinking wine, and you find that you're physically and/or sexually very attracted to each other, you might not find out the important issues until much later. By not discussing "who" you are and what you want up front only serves to waste time and create potential heartbreak and disappointment later, if you are clear that you are dating to marry. While this may seem fairly obvious, it's not. And it is a radical departure from how people date today.

Goals are tied to your dreams and your vision: where you want to live, how you want to live, the things you'd like to accomplish, where you'd like to go, what you'd like to be remembered for, the how and the why of actively being you, and how you see your future. By articulating your goals, you'll be able to find someone who will share and/or support your vision and goals, which will lead to a directed life of partnership.

3. Learn how to date for marriage by having meaningful conversations.

Dating for marriage is a passionate pursuit between mature people with clear vision. It is about having meaningful conversations, and when real potential exists, it's very exciting. It's stimulating and inspiring to discuss possibilities up front rather than remain in mystery.

When you release yourself from the shackles of destructive and time-wasting dating strategies, you'll find yourself refreshed, inspired, and excited about your journey.

As I mentioned, dating for marriage is when two marriage-minded people are having meaningful conversations (not random selection: "Oh, you're cute! You like sushi and moonlit, romantic dinners? Me too! Great, it must be love.").

When dating for marriage, you are clear about who you are and what you are looking for, so you can be warm, open, and transparent. You can meet people and not worry about apparently conflicting details like, "Oh, but he or she looks good on paper" when your gut tells you that someone is not a match. You can be comfortable on a coffee date without looking over your shoulder wondering if you are missing out on someone better. You will express your marriage goal clearly and enroll your friends, family, and community in your vision (in the same way you might express your career goals)[4]. You will date with faith and confidence by conducting yourself like a marriage-minded individual.

You'll discuss who you are, not what you do. When? From the first conversation! Yes, that's right, from the very first conversation. When dating for marriage, you'll articulate that you are marriage-minded among other important elements of who you are. You'll discuss core issues that make up who you are. You'll discuss your family, your background, your passions; ask meaningful questions; discuss the future you envision, how you'd like to live, and your values; and you'll listen for what the other person is about. You'll compare and contrast.

You'll discuss your dreams, hopes, aspirations, and plans—what your vision is for your life, your future, and your sensibilities. You'll use the forms and exercises in Part II, the Attract section (especially Chapter 7), to define and articulate it all for yourself. Discussing interests won't get you there. The strongest marriages

---

4 Many singles proudly share their career or education goals with others and pursue these goals with rigor, but not their marriage goal. Because they've had bad experiences, they hide what they really want and keep it a secret. However, by enrolling others in their marriage goals, they would be in a better position to achieve that which they want most.

are made up of life partners who share a similar worldview and common vision, values, and goals (and who are passionate best friends).

We'll discuss all of these elements in the pages ahead. You'll read practical and refreshing dating tips and slogans that can be used as tools to keep you on the Meet to Marry path. No more mystery dating! No dating people whose goals are unknown! You'll learn to identify the top three ways to choose a spouse, skills that most people don't know. If you're able to make just this one distinction from reading *Meet to Marry,* your dating future will significantly change! You will:

✓ Make a Commitment to Yourself.
✓ Create your Dating Plan of Action.
✓ Follow the Tips and Slogans for Dating to Marry.

Along the way, you'll read real-life case studies and success stories, as well as stories from my life leading up to finding and marrying Michael eight years ago.

Date to Marry Tip: Timing is everything— this is the perfect time to meet your ideal spouse!

You are a unique, remarkable person. Your life's journey has brought you right to this point. At the same time, your "perfect match" has also been traveling a similar, exceptional path, readying himself or herself for you. Hold no regrets about the past—regrets just drag you down!

"Timing is perfect" is your new mantra. Whatever your history, know this to be true: you made the best choices you could at the time, and you responded as well as you were able. You lived, you loved, and you learned.

2
Create Your Own "Dating" Reality

I was a statistic. There I was, being told over and over by nice, well-meaning people that I was more likely to be struck by lightning twice than to get married over the age of thirty-five. After all, the competition out there was unforgiving, and time was running out. I couldn't get the image of Marisa Tomei in *My Cousin Vinny*, angrily tapping her foot about her "biological clock ticking like this," out of my thoughts. I pictured myself as a cartoon time bomb, the fuse lit and hissing closer and closer. Panic settled into my daily life, and I almost succumbed to the belief that I would always find myself in the lonely, unsatisfying relationships I was familiar with. I was terrified I might never find meaningful love and have my own family.

You too may have become disillusioned in your life about the possibility of ever making a connection. Many singles attribute it to "the lousy dating sites" and "the lame singles events." Regardless of where you live, you may think that you would be better off dating someplace else. Daters on the Upper West Side of Manhattan are convinced that "everyone knows everyone," and that if they were just in Miami it would all be better. And, of course, the singles in Miami think they need to move to New York or Paris or someplace else.

Many men have expressed concerns to me that the only women they meet are shallow, unrealistic, and closed off; that they are looking for wealthy, handsome guys who play golf and drive fancy cars. With unrealistic expectations of income and stature, these women don't want a real person: "They don't see me," many men say.

I met a group of six women in their forties, affectionately known as "the singles," in a beach community on Long Island. They come back to the beach, year in and year out, with no change in status. They shared their dating experiences with me, and the consistency of their mantras is telling: "The quality of men is awful," "The men just aren't interested in us," and the ever-present, "I have a great attitude, but I never seem to meet the right one." It is undeniable: most singles actually have the same complaints. These include:

- I've been at it for years and still can't meet "the one."
- I wasted too much time in the wrong relationships.
- I hate Internet dating! You never know who really wants to get married.
- Singles events are filled with losers.
- Everyone knows everyone here. I should go somewhere else.
- It's a "meat market" where I live.
- I waited so long and focused on my career. What did it get me?
- I lived with someone and found out later that he/she didn't want to get married.
- Where are the serious women and men who want partnership and to build a home?

If you are sincere and are doing all of the right things, but you find you're attracting random people, or people who don't "get it" or "get you," then it's time to look under the hood of dating to understand that *what you think and how you feel directly relates to what you have and what you attract into your life.* There's no hiding it.

Tuning in to Your Hidden Frequency: You Attract What You Send Out

As human beings, we have a limited perception of reality. We believe that if we can't see something or we don't have physical evidence of it, it doesn't exist. For example, although you can't see them, microscopic molecules make up the very book you are holding in your hands. When you make a cell phone call, you can't see the signal flying past you, but you know you've made the connection.

You may believe that the singles events are lousy, that it's really difficult to connect and find the kind of person you are looking for. You may believe that there is no one worth dating and that you need to move to another city or town. You may even believe that there's just no one out there for you.

As you read on, I ask that you have an open mind and consider the possibility that the reason you haven't met "the one" yet has nothing to do with anything "out there." In dating, as in life, what you think is true may not be true, and creating your own *new* reality is the foundation for having the life you want. *Your future is in your hands and in your thoughts.*

What you think (both consciously and unconsciously) is the primary determining factor in what and who shows up for you. Thoughts have energy, and you attract what it is that you feel you deserve. So, if you are thinking, "Dating is a waste of my time," or "There's no one to date," that can, in fact, be your self-created reality. You also attract what you project, just like a mirror. For example, if you are cynical, you can attract cynical people into your life (the *opposite* of what you say you want). The principles involved here are laws of nature—principles found operating in the physics of the universe.

Like many people, I was smart, attractive, and successful, yet I consistently attracted the wrong people, as you read earlier.

Why? Was it really because there was no one out there for me? Because the dating sites were lousy? Because the singles events were terrible? Because there were no "normal" guys?

Wouldn't you agree that what often appears to be true isn't really true, and that there are forces at work that cannot be seen, as in the book and the cell phone examples? And so it is with dating.

My unconscious "story" (the one I carried around in my head) was that there was something wrong with me. Sure enough, all of the guys I attracted reinforced that story. The evidence was that mismatched, emotionally unavailable guys kept showing up. I attracted them. If there were a hundred guys in the room, I would attract the unhealthy ones, the "wrong" ones. Chemically, on an energy level, I would attract them to me, and my radar was targeted to satisfy my never-ending, subconscious story about myself. These guys didn't outwardly project "I'm not emotionally available," but that is what they were.

Because that was my energy—unconsciously or not—that was the reality I created for myself. And on the surface, it looked like the truth, based on the evidence. So when the evidence says, "There's no one to date," "The dating sites are lousy," "Men are commitment-phobes," or "Women are shallow," is it "the truth," or is it simply what you attracted in the first place? When I attracted the wrong guys who reinforced my story and the way I felt about myself, did it mean there were no great men out there? *How can that be possible?*

After all, other people were meeting great men. In reality, they were out there, but not for me. Of course not. Like a magnet, I was attracting what I felt I deserved. You've probably heard the expression, "He/she has good vibes." Good thoughts and positive energy attract the same energy.

So when you don't know yourself how your past affects your current reality, what you want and need in a spouse, and you harbor negativity, skepticism, fear and upset related to dating, you are actually attracting that same energy. For example, if you say you want to meet someone warm, kind, and welcoming, but you are *being* negative, skeptical, and judgmental, you are likely going to attract someone who is just like the way you are *being* rather than what you are *saying*. When the attraction is mysterious and chemical, the connection feels real. So I ask you, *what kind of people are you attracting?* If you do a lot of the right things, like dress well, look great, go on a lot of dates, and put yourself in all of the right places, but deep down you have unconscious stories about yourself, negative vibes, skepticism, misconceptions, and confusion, do you think it will make a difference?

This is the "Dating Epidemic." And until I realized what was actually going on, I was doomed to continue attracting men who would reinforce the story I had about myself—and I didn't even know it! I had to change—to wake up and have a breakthrough—and take personal responsibility for who I was *being* in my life. The truth is:

I had to Be the one to find The One.

And when I did, my energy changed and my life changed.

The wrong ones stopped showing up! Now, on the outside, it appeared to be true. There was *evidence*: no good men, they're all lousy, and so on. There was lots of evidence to prove this. And to observers, it sure looked like I was okay and they were not. In our society, those bookshelves filled with dating guides and those TV talk shows and movies on the subject of dating all reinforce the wrong thinking.

So I ask you: In a city like New York City, with more than 8 million people, how can a person date for more than ten years and not find their perfect match? Is this problem external, something to do with the environment and the conditions around them? Or is the explanation—the *cause*—within you?

Marriage, Media, and Stereotypes

One thing is certain about marriage: people have strong opinions about it. They are either running toward it or running away—far away—from it. You won't find many people without a clear, personal view of this social and cultural institution.

What is it about marriage that elicits passionate discussion of its merits and pitfalls? As the most fundamental unit of human civilization, some form of marriage has existed since well before the beginning of recorded history. In every age, marriage has been as much of a cultural fascination as it was a cornerstone of society.

Marriage is a central theme to countless important writers and artists throughout time, from Sophocles and Euripides to

Shakespeare, Rembrandt, Molière, Jane Austen, Henri Rousseau, Amedeo Modigliani, Marc Chagall, Frida Kahlo, and many others. To this day, the amount of media attention on dating and marriage is mind-blowing. Books, movies, pop songs, and reality shows are just some of the media devoted to telling us how to be more desirable to the opposite sex, how to win a spouse, and how to keep them happy once we've got one. From the reality show about how to marry a millionaire to the not-so-funny Super Bowl ads, there's no shortage of stereotypical and superficial messages about love. Whatever the level of our individual media consumption, we cannot help being bombarded with images and messages about marriage. Whether we like it or not, *we're susceptible to absorbing the unrealistic stereotypes the media projects.*

Movies, books, and television all contribute to the message that "love is chemical." It's based on good looks, common interests, and attraction. Stereotypes are alive and well in the movies, and along with television, they are perhaps the most powerful influence on our perception of gender. Men are portrayed either as commitment-phobic, sports-addicted beer drinkers (Vince Vaughn in *The Break-Up*) or as romantic saviors who magically arrive on the proverbial white horse (Richard Gere in *Pretty Woman*). Women are portrayed as either dumb sex kittens to be taken care of (the Marilyn Monroes), or strong, often hardened, career-driven women to be tamed (the Katharine Hepburns).

The movie *The Ugly Truth* attempts to reveal the gospel that men "cannot be trained." Abby Richter (Katherine Heigl) plays a single, attractive, Type-A television producer who wants to marry an enlightened, sensitive, and caring guy. Mike Chadway (Gerard Butler), an overconfident, chauvinistic TV celebrity, becomes her dating Cyrano, teaching her that in order to land a man, she needs to dress sexier, act sexier, and be way less intelligent. With a new, alluring facade, straight off the cover of *Cosmo*, her love interest's eyes pop out of his head and he falls in love with her. But in the end, is he really the person she wanted? Will women be happy donning push-up bras and high heels, trying to learn to love sports? Sure, we all need to put our best foot forward and be great partners, but with messages like "Don't turn men into women," and "Just give a man what he wants and needs," what is society telling us? Are women becoming convinced that they must change to suit a man and thus willingly discard their identities in the process?

The messages are certainly confusing. What is the truth? Are men two-dimensional, untrainable slobs who tuck tail and run at the first mention of commitment? Are they unevolved creatures or single-minded seducers? Are women just clueless victims? Are they hardened idealists, competing like men in a man's world? Or are they whiny complainers, resigned to believing that there are no marriage-worthy men out there? *Because of these stereotypical and superficial messages, singles are not connecting—and they are not connecting in record numbers. What is the disconnect?*

Take the Marriage Readiness Quiz

The first tool of the program is the Marriage Readiness Quiz, which identifies ten important criteria of marriage readiness. By carefully evaluating your situation, you can identify the areas in which you've got a healthy outlook versus areas in which you may have blind spots (You'll learn more about blind spots and blockages in Chapter 3). You can use this information to isolate the areas where you have blockages, lack of clarity, or where you are not taking appropriate action—all of which can keep you from your ultimate goal of having a fulfilling marriage and partnership.

Answer the questions truthfully in order to identify crucial problem areas. Do not answer with what you think is the right answer; rather, answer according to what is true for you now to get the full benefit.

1. **Do you believe you will meet your ideal marriage partner?**
   a. Yes, I am confident that I will attract my ideal marriage partner. I have self-confidence, I have faith that timing is crucial, and I make an effort to put myself in the right places and situations.
   b. I believe I will, but I think it will take time, patience, hard work, and a lot of compromise.
   c. I think that almost anyone can be right if both are willing to work at it.
   d. I guess it's possible, but I've had a lot of bad experiences.

2. **Are you clear about the kind of relationship you would like to have and the kind of person you would like to meet?**
   a. Yes, I have a clear vision of how I would like to feel in a relationship

and what my partner will be like. I know myself, my needs, and what I want for the future.

b. I have an idea, but I could use more clarity about how to really know if someone is right for me.

c. I am specifically looking for someone of a certain age with certain interests, and I don't plan to deviate from that picture.

d. I don't really know what I'm looking for, so I will date anyone and see how it goes.

3. **Do you make dating a priority?**

a. I do. I understand that since I am committed to getting married as one of my life goals, dating must be a top priority. I allot time every week in my schedule, even if and when I am very busy.

b. My schedule is hectic, and I squeeze dating and dating activities in when I can. It's sporadic and can be inconsistent.

c. I am not comfortable with "scheduling" dating time and dating-related activities. I believe it will just happen organically.

d. I can't remember the last time I went on a date.

4. **Do you spend time with former spouses or dates that didn't work out romantically?**

a. Spending time with exes can block me energetically. If a date tells me, "Let's be friends," I am reminded at that point that I am committed to finding my future spouse, and there is no reason to spend time with him/her.

b. I mostly spend time with friends of the same gender, but sometimes if a date doesn't work out, I turn that person into a friend.

c. I have a lot of friends I formerly dated, and I even give them advice about their dating life. I think it's fine, and you never know if things will turn around.

   d. Former girlfriends/boyfriends are fun to spend time with and
      keep me busy while I'm looking for "the one."

5. Are you "over" your past romances?

   a. Yes, all relationships from the past are "closed books," and
      we have all moved on to our own separate paths.

   b. There is one former love who I still think about, and I know I should
      "complete that chapter." With everyone else, it's definitely over.

   c. I can't seem to let go of a past love, so I keep the door open, just in case.

   d. I don't want to close the door with my ex, since you never know.

6. Do you feel good about yourself, your appearance, your attitude, and how you present yourself?

   a. I do. I take care of myself and do my best to be healthy and happy. I
      think I present myself in the best light possible, and when I feel good
      about myself, I find that I attract good things into my life.

   b. I feel pretty good about my appearance, but I could definitely do more in
      terms of presentation. If I did, I'm sure I would feel more self-confident.

   c. I feel insecure in several areas, and I know it keeps my energy low. I
      could use some advice, but I don't know where to begin.

   d. I'm happy the way I am, and I don't have time to pay attention
      to such things. My partner will like me the way I am.

7. How would you classify your life as a whole, now, while you are single?

   a. I have a full life in all areas with a great support system of friends,
      family, and interests. My life will be complemented all the more
      when I meet my ideal spouse. In the meantime, I continue to develop
      myself and am ready to welcome him/her when it happens.

   b. My life is great in most areas, but I do feel a little stuck and very self-
      conscious about being single when "everyone else is married."

c. I feel somewhat lonely and depressed, and I sometimes wonder what's wrong with me . . . and if "it" will ever happen.

d. I hate being single and need someone in my life to feel happy.

8. I believe I can meet my ideal marriage partner in the following ways and under the following conditions:

a. I am open to meeting someone in a variety of ways, and I don't judge different venues based on past experiences. I understand that my future spouse is also searching for me, and our paths can cross in unexpected ways, including Internet dating, introductions, chance meetings, or at a random event.

b. I've had some bad experiences with certain kinds of events, so I don't go to them anymore.

c. I only date by introduction—I don't trust the Internet because I've only met losers on dating sites. I also don't feel comfortable talking to strangers, and I won't open myself up to them.

d. I believe my ideal mate will find me somehow, so I don't have to "put myself out there."

9. I handle my dates as follows:

a. I meet a first date for coffee after first speaking on the phone to be sure there is a foundation for a meeting. I treat a date as a special person, and I respect their time as I do my own. I give them my full attention, and I end dates with clear communication, even when the person is not a "match."

b. On a date I'm a pretty active listener, but if after a little while I feel he/she isn't "the one," I tend to drift away or just talk about myself.

c. I am considerate to my dates, but in reality I try to keep things vague so I can carefully think about the situation.

d. If I'm not interested in a particular date, I zone out and even look around the room to see who else might be interesting.

10. The reason I am now dating to marry is:

 a. I know myself well, and I know what I am looking for in a marriage partner. I am genuinely ready to share my life with someone in a wonderful, committed, and loving relationship.

 b. The time has come. I want to share my life with someone and experience what it would be like to take care of someone else and also be taken care of.

 c. I think I am ready and I want to take the big leap into new waters.

 d. I don't want to be alone anymore and I want someone to take care of me.

RESULTS: Count the total number of A's, B's, C's, and D's.

 A. _____

 B. _____

 C. _____

 D. _____

If most of your answers were A's, *congratulations*! You are in a great place, and you're ready to meet and welcome the "right one" into your life. You are open-minded, self-aware, and understand that so much in life revolves around timing. Because you live a full, rich life, you are happy from the inside and ready to attract your future spouse, wherever he/she might be.

If your answers were not all A's, you're in good company too—you're ready to grow and have breakthroughs. You are in the right place at the right time!

Getting to the A's

In the Marriage Readiness Quiz, "the A's have it," because they reflect marriage readiness and healthy thinking. If you chose B, C, and D answers, you may have blind spots or blockages that manifest themselves in fear, negativity, cynicism, inaction in varying degrees, or not being in touch with your "dating reality." The B, C, and D answers reveal the means by which you approach your life, views that are not as powerful motivators as they need to be. As you move closer to the A's, the healthier your thinking will be and the more open and ready you'll be to welcoming "the one" you are looking for into your life.

The gap between the A's and the other answers shows us where the growth needs to happen. The Meet to Marry coaching program is about getting to the A's. Use all three sections and tools of Assess, Attract, and Act to uncover blind spots or blockages that may be keeping you from your dream, gain clarity and articulate your vision, and finally, get into action that's consistent with your vision. Using the coaching program's tools, you can get to the A's and have those breakthrough "Ah ha!" moments along the way. The following analysis gives you the opportunity to critically reflect on your answers.

Quiz Question No. 1:
Do you believe you will meet your ideal marriage partner?

Question 1 of the Marriage Readiness Quiz addresses your beliefs and attitudes about dating, marriage, and your state of readiness.

Answer A: *Yes, I am confident that I will attract my ideal marriage partner. I have self-confidence, I have faith that timing is crucial, and I make an effort to put myself in the right places and situations.*

The healthy answer presents the right combination of confidence, faith, timing, and action in support of your life and your vision.

Answer B: *I believe I will, but I think it will take time, patience, hard work, and a lot of compromise.*

Answer B is a value judgment. It simply isn't the truth. It may be what your current experience has led you to believe, but the past definitely does not dictate the future. It may take time and patience to meet "the right one," but hard work implies drudgery, negativity, and effort. Consider that what you say and believe creates your reality. A more positive and empowering alternative would be to consider changing the context of dating from being hard and difficult to something that is exciting, vital, and faith-inspired, which will lead you to action.

Answer C: *I think that almost anyone can be right if both are willing to work at it.*

Answer C indicates that dating is random, and that with work, any two people can make it together. It is possible, but it's not very likely. Every person in this world is unique, with unique needs and backgrounds. Not everyone is going to be an "ideal fit" for everyone else. In fact, it's more likely that "ideal fits" are a rare occurrence indeed, because most of us operate without preparation and guidance. A more productive approach is to identify and clarify your emotional needs, wants, desires, and dreams, and then to proceed to use your criteria to look for someone who will be an ideal match for you.

Answer D: *I guess it's possible, but I've had a lot of bad experiences.*

Answer D is negative and cynical. It is repetitive, but it's worth saying again: The past does not dictate the future. If you see dating as negative, it will be negative and unsatisfying. However, one bad experience (or even several bad experiences) doesn't mean the next experience will be negative. If you have a bad meal, you don't stop eating, right?

Quiz Question No. 2: *Are you clear about the kind of relationship you would like to have and the kind of person you would like to meet?*

Question 2 addresses your clarity of vision and your knowledge of your own emotional needs.

Answer A: *Yes, I have a clear vision of how I would like to feel in a relationship and what my partner will be like. I know myself, my needs, and what I want for the future.*

This healthy answer comes from a place of lucidity about the kind of person you'd like to attract as a life partner. If you know yourself and have given deep thought to what you want in your life, you'll be more likely to attract the kind of person you'd like to meet.

Answer B: *I have an idea, but I could use more clarity about how to really know if someone is right for me.*

If you chose B, you are in a great spot. The following exercises in this book will help you attain just the clarity you need to create your own vision of what a fulfilling marriage partner will look like.

Answer C: *I am specifically looking for someone of a certain age with certain interests, and I don't plan to deviate from that picture.*

If you chose C, you're not being realistic. By restricting yourself so much, you could be sabotaging your own efforts, turning a blind eye to a wonderful person who could be great for you. Take a close look at the reality of your present situation and consider expanding your options. Being open to meeting someone whose "packaging" is different than your fixed ideas may find you a world of happiness.

As an example, when I was thirty-five, I only wanted to meet someone without children. I later realized that my perspective wasn't healthy, and it was high time for a reality check. In my situation, I was much more likely to meet a pool of men in their forties who were divorced. If I were to eliminate men without children, I would be closing myself off to many possibilities. Families come to us in many ways and shapes, and there is no shortage of love I could offer and receive, if I were more open to doing so.

Answer D: *I don't really know what I am looking for, so I will date anyone and see how it goes.*

To win the game, you need to know the parameters. There are many elements that make a great match, as you will learn in upcoming chapters. If you approach dating to marry randomly, your results will likely be random. With this book in your hands, you are in a great place to learn about yourself, and you'll soon be in a position to attract someone who will be perfect for you.

Quiz Question No. 3: *Do you make dating a priority?*

Question 3 asks if your actions are consistent with your vision.

Answer A: *I do. I understand that since I am committed to getting married as one of my life goals, dating must be a top priority. I allot time every week in my schedule, even if and when I am very busy.*

Answering with A demonstrates a success-oriented sense of commitment: your actions are consistent with your goals, and you have a winning approach.

Answer B: *My schedule is hectic, and I squeeze dating and dating activities in when I can. It's sporadic and can be inconsistent.*

It's great that you are dating, but if you make it a priority, as well as proactively identifying who and what you ideally want in your life, you'll see amazing results.

Answer C: *I am not comfortable with "scheduling" dating time and dating-related activities. I believe it will just happen organically.*

If you have a wait-and-see method, you are not approaching dating as effectively as you could. The Dating Plan of Action in Chapter 8 makes dating fun and exciting. Successful people do what unsuccessful people won't do.

Answer D: *I can't remember the last time I went on a date.*

Your actions are not consistent with your vision. Implementing the Dating Plan of Action in Chapter 8 is critical, if getting married is, indeed, a serious goal for your immediate future.

Quiz Question No. 4: *Do you spend time with former spouses or dates that didn't work out romantically?*

Question 4 addresses both your availability and your level of commitment to your goals.

Answer A: *Spending time with exes can block me energetically. If a date tells me, "Let's be friends," I am reminded at that point that I am committed to finding my future spouse, and there is no reason to spend time with him/her.*

That's the winning attitude! Answer A indicates you have healthy boundaries and a clear sense of what you want out of dating to marry.

Answer B: *I mostly spend time with friends of the same gender, but sometimes if a date doesn't work out, I turn that person into a friend.*

It could be beneficial to ask yourself, "Why? Do I need more friends?" Try just being friends with supportive people of the same gender and watch what happens. When you turn a former date into a friend, what is your real intention?

Answer C: *I have a lot of friends I formerly dated, and I even give them advice about their dating life. I think it's fine, and you never know if things will turn around.*

When men and women, especially those who've dated in the

past, are just friends, it is still "intimate," because of the nature of men and women. It just is. As an experiment, tell your friends of the opposite sex that you must take a break from them while dating for marriage. With this mind-set, the next person of the opposite sex you spend time with may be your future spouse, the person you'll be building a life with. Take this challenge and watch the results.

Answer D: *Former girlfriends/boyfriends are fun to spend time with and keep me busy while I'm looking for "the one."*

Again, when men and women are just friends, it's still "intimate" by nature. A friend of mine rejected this advice at first, until she had lunch with a male friend. He shared with her his dating and sexual exploits, and it brought her down. She then decided to take a break. If you are serious about dating for marriage, you won't have time to just "stay busy" passing time. Remember, time is the only thing you can't get back.

Quiz Question No. 5: *Are you "over" your past romances?*

Question 5 asks if your energy is free to welcome someone "perfect" into your life.

Answer A: *Yes, all relationships from the past are "closed books," and we have all moved on to our own separate paths.*

Awesome. When I said good-bye to an ex, it set us both free, and the result was that I met Michael. I now have a life that is beyond my wildest expectations. Anything else postpones your life.

Answer B: *There is one former love who I still think about, and I know I should "complete that chapter." With everyone else, it's definitely over.*

Thinking about even one former love can clog your energy and not leave room for "the right one." Is there someone you are thinking about?

Answer C: *I can't seem to let go of a past love, so I keep the door open, just in case.*

You are not leaving room for new love in your life. Do you really need a security blanket? No! Let go and be free to allow new love into your life. Be happy and get closure so you can move on.

Answer D: *I don't want to close the door with any ex, since you never know.*

This is unhealthy thinking. The relationship is over and you haven't been able to accept it. You deserve to be with your perfect partner, which this person is not. Make room for new love in your life. If you don't achieve closure, you are standing still. Ask yourself, "What am I willing to do to get what I want?"

Quiz Question No. 6: *Do you feel good about yourself, your appearance, your attitude, and how you present yourself?*

Question 6 asks if you are self-confident and feeling your best.

Answer A: *I do. I take care of myself and do my best to be healthy and happy. I think I present myself in the best light possible, and* *when I feel good about myself, I find that I attract good things into my life.*

You have a great and healthy attitude!

Answer B: *I feel pretty good about my appearance, but I could definitely do more in terms of presentation. If I did, I'm sure I would feel more self-confident.*

Love yourself and how you look and feel. (See the Date to Marry Tips in Chapter 8 for more detail.) With slight adjustments, your self-esteem can soar.

Answer C: *I feel insecure in several areas, and I know it keeps my energy low. I could use some advice, but I don't know where to begin.*

It's time to discover how making minor adjustments to your outer appearance can affect how you feel about yourself. Taking good care of yourself is as much for your health and well-being as it is for aesthetics. When you feel good about how you look and feel, you'll resonates with positivity. Remember, to find *the one*, you have to *be* the one. First and foremost, you need to feel good about yourself.

Answer D: *I'm happy the way I am, and I don't have time to pay attention to such things. My partner will like me the way I am.*

Your ideal spouse will like, love, and accept you, but you do need to put your best foot forward. Why the resistance? Once again, take to heart: "Be your best and feel your best! Love yourself and how you look and feel." (See the Date to Marry Tips in Chapter 8) It sounds like you have a blind spot in the area of "living in reality," so consider exploring why you are inflexible in this area.

Quiz Question No. 7: *How would you classify your life as a whole, now, while you are single?*

Question 7 asks if you are leading a happy and full life or if you are feeling needy. Remember: attachment is the enemy of happiness.

Answer A: *I have a full life in all areas with a great support system of friends, family, and interests. My life will be complemented all the more when I meet my ideal spouse. In the meantime, I continue to develop myself and am ready to welcome him/her when it happens.*

This response shows you have a healthy sense of self and a level of true marriage readiness. You are obviously ready to welcome "the right one" into your life.

Answer B: *My life is great in most areas, but I do feel a little stuck and very conscious about being single when "everyone else is married."*

Great! Consider that you are exactly where you need to be at this very moment. If you feel like you are ready to get married, get into action. Know that someone is preparing himself or herself for you. The only people you'd want to compare yourself to are people you don't know.

Answer C: *I feel somewhat lonely and depressed, and I sometimes wonder what's wrong with me . . . and if "it" will ever happen.*

You are a very special and lovable person, and you can change your feelings and circumstances. What you are feeling may be an attachment to the past. Thinking positively will create positive results. Get into action and create your future. Be your own best friend and advocate.

Answer D: *I hate being single and need someone in my life to feel happy.*

Being needy is not a healthy place to be when searching for a relationship. Desperation and negativity will only attract desperation and negativity. Your job is to "*be* the one," and this is done by being as healthy, happy, and complete as you can possibly be.

Quiz Question No. 8: *I believe I can meet my ideal partner in the following ways and under the following conditions:*

Question 8 asks if you are open to various possibilities and the miracles and surprises that life brings.

Answer A: *I am open to meeting someone in a variety of ways, and I don't judge different venues based on past experiences. I understand that my future spouse is also searching for me, and our paths can cross in unexpected ways, including Internet dating, introductions, chance meetings, or at a random event.*

This response is healthy, because it's open-minded and focused on using multiple avenues for success. You are free to be without constraints, you have a great attitude, and you're demonstrating faith.

Answer B: *I've had some bad experiences with certain kinds of events, so I don't go to them anymore.*

While upsetting, bad experiences can be overcome with an

attitude adjustment. Because an experience was negative, it doesn't mean that future events will be negative. Choose to think positively and you'll find the good in all of your experiences.

Answer C: *I only date by introduction—I don't trust the Internet because I've only met losers on dating sites. I also don't feel comfortable talking to strangers, and I won't open myself up to them.*

Attitude is everything. The Internet opens up many new doors and possibilities for meeting people. When used properly with proper screening, your range of possibilities can open up in a vast new way.

Answer D: *I believe my ideal mate will find me somehow, so I don't have to "put myself out there."*

It's true that your soul mate is out there, but if you don't put yourself out there, how will he or she find you? It is naive, wishful thinking to believe it will just happen by staying home.

Quiz Question No. 9: *I handle my dates as follows:*

Question 9 asks how you relate to the people you date.

Answer A: *I treat a date as a special person, and I respect their time as I do my own. I give them my full attention, and I end dates with clear communication, even when the person is not a "match."*

Answering A shows that you have a keen eye for evaluating dates to see if they complement your ideal vision. Regardless of whether the person you are dating is "the one," it is respectful to give that person your full attention. You also recognize the value of dating with clarity.

Answer B: *On a date, I'm a pretty active listener. But if after a little while I feel he or she isn't "the one," I tend to drift away or just talk about myself.*

To avoid the above scenario, keep your first dates short, not more than thirty minutes or so. Set the stage by letting the person know that you'd like to meet for coffee "to see if there is anything there." You will know after a short coffee date if the person is someone you'd like to see again.

Answer C: *I am considerate to my dates, but in reality I try to keep things vague so I can carefully think about the situation.*

Life is short, and finding a fulfilling marriage partner is what you said you want—nothing less! There is no point in being vague about your objectives during a date. After completing this program, you will have the wisdom and confidence to know how to end dates with clarity, as well as the ability to know if the person is someone you should see again.

Answer D: *If I'm not interested in a particular date, I zone out and even look around the room to see who else might be interesting.*

There is never a reason to be rude. By keeping your dates "short and sweet," you can be kind and respectful to the person you are meeting. By being considerate to others, it will boomerang right back to you into your life!

Quiz Question No. 10:

The reason I am now dating to marry is:

Question 10 asks you to reflect on whether or not you are ready to marry with a big vision. (And the point is: have the biggest vision possible for your life.)

Answer A: *I know myself well, and I know what I am looking for in a marriage partner. I am genuinely ready to share my life with someone in a wonderful, committed, and loving relationship.*

By answering A, it's clear that you're ready to realize your vision and embark on your ideal marriage.

Answer B: *The time has come. I want to share my life with someone and experience what it would be like to take care of someone else and also be taken care of.*

Taking care of someone and being taken care of is only part of the picture. When you are marriage-ready, you'll have clarity about what you want and need in a relationship.

Answer C: *I think I am ready and I want to take the big leap into new waters.*

Thinking you're ready and being ready are two different states of consciousness. By doing some honest self-reflection and carefully following the material in this book, your "marriage readiness" will generate a confidence and assuredness worthy of you.

Answer D: *I don't want to be alone anymore and I want someone to take care of me.*

"Neediness" is not a powerful place to be when looking for a relationship. Knowing yourself and your own "stuff"—being as happy, healthy, and complete as possible—is a much better, more advisable approach.

Have a Breakthrough:
Getting to the A's Exercise:

Now that you've completed the quiz, you're ready to reflect on your answers. Note the questions for which you didn't choose A answers. For those questions, what actions or steps would you take to get closer to A responses?

Use the following questions to prompt your response:

- What did you notice about the question? (i.e. agreement, recognition, challenge, etc.)
- What is the feeling related to your answer? (i.e. resistance, resignation, sadness, etc.)
- What could you change or do to have a breakthrough in getting to the A answer?
- What are you willing to do?
- What do you think you should do?

Date to Marry Tip: Maintain a positive attitude and sense of humor.

This is an exciting adventure you are embarking on in pursuing your search for a life partner. Know that each "wrong" person you meet will lead you closer to "the one." It's best to be lighthearted in your approach and see the humor and good points in all of your experiences.

If you go to a "bad" singles event, don't let it get you down. See it as it is—just an experience—and forge ahead. Don't add meaning where there is none. If you hear your negative voice sneaking in, tell it, "Thank you for sharing," and move on to the next experience. Attend the next event (don't close your options needlessly), as maybe the one you are looking for will be there, too.

Attitude Is Everything

Dr. Viktor Frankl (1905–97), a Viennese psychotherapist, spent three long years in Hitler's concentration camps. He lost his parents, brother, and pregnant wife to the "Final Solution," but did not lose his vision of human dignity.

In the first half of his bestselling book, *Man's Search for Meaning,* he describes his harrowing experience in the camps and considers how it was that some of the prisoners seemed to be able to transcend their surroundings. He writes, "We who lived in concentration camps can remember the men who walked through the huts comforting others, giving away their last piece of bread . . . they offer sufficient proof that everything can be taken from a man but one thing: the last of the human freedoms—to choose one's attitude in any given set of circumstances, to choose one's own way."

He concludes that even in the most severe suffering, the human being can find meaning and thus hope. Frankl references Nietzsche: "He who has a *why* to live can bear with almost any *how*." In the end, Frankl came to this conclusion: "The truth— that love is the ultimate and the highest goal to which man can aspire."

3

Blind Spots and Breakthroughs

I was sitting with someone I'll call Kathy, who was describing her dating situation and woes. She was proudly telling me how open, loving, and self-aware she is. Kathy described being tired of dating men she needs to train, men who are beneath her. She wants a grown-up, a real man who would be her equal, but over and over, Kathy said, the same guys keep showing up. "Why can't I meet someone like me?" she asked.

But from the moment of our encounter, my impression of Kathy was anything but loving. She complained about the neighbors, described how she didn't approve of her family, how she is not on speaking terms with them, and several other revealing complaints, all expressed with a smile.

In her mind, Kathy is clear that she is "fine," and she definitely believes that the problem is outside of herself, that there is no one worthy of her to date. She has *evidence*, right? Warm, loving, mature guys never show up. She believes with complete certainty that there are no good men out there, and certainly no one for her, and if there are, where are they?

This is a blind spot.

Like so many others I encounter, Kathy is a person who is totally sincere about her desire to meet someone. When asked if she is marriage-ready, she said she's been ready for ten years (since her divorce), and that no one is more ready than she. Kathy explained that she is a trained therapist and knows herself well from "all of the work" she has done on herself. She told me that her own therapist (reinforcing her flawed thinking) has been telling her that she is correct: that the special man she wants to find will be one in 2 million, because Kathy is the epitome of loving-kindness. And because she believes him, she won't even know that she needs to take personal responsibility for her life—and that is sad.

Getting back to Kathy's original question—"Why can't I meet someone like me?"—the answer is: she has. And she keeps meeting them.

If you've been looking for "the one" and dating for a while, and you see patterns that are not serving you, this discussion can be very revealing, but only if you are open to it. As human beings, we were born into this blind-spot trap. The good news is that through healthy thinking and developing greater self-awareness, our blind spots can be uncovered. With a lighthearted approach, let's begin.

What Is a Blind Spot?

Like the part of the road you can't see in your rearview mirror when driving, a blind spot is something about yourself of which you are not consciously aware. It's there, but you can't see it. People in your life may know what your blind spots are, but you don't. Typically, you're the last one to know. By uncovering a blind spot and bringing it to your awareness, you can finally arrive at a place of inspiration that leads to action. Becoming *unstuck* is a direct result of uncovering this new information. Jumping into action allows for miraculous changes in your life.

Warning Signs of a Blind Spot

Blind spots can manifest when you complain and make excuses about people or situations. The irony about blind spots is that other people can recognize them right away. As for us, though, they are hidden from our view. When you are unaware of the behavior and believe the external event is causing the problem, this is a blind spot. Until you uncover these blind spots, they will continue to keep you from your happiness. Some warning signs that a blind spot is in action include statements like:

All women are . . .

All men are . . .

There is no one left to date.

Everyone out there is lousy.

Men are afraid of commitment.

Women don't get me.

There are no good guys to connect with.

The scene is awful.

I really do my best to be out there, but . . .

It's a meat market.

It's a bloodbath.

When we cannot (or will not) find the true causes to events that take place in our lives, we pin the blame on anything outside of ourselves. *The hard truth is that the real causes never come from outside of us.* They come from within. That means that the real solutions never come from outside of us either.

The key to having the life of your dreams is *inside* of you. Just like you can see solutions to so many of your friends' "obvious" problems while they walk around clueless, the outside observer can easily see what we are oblivious to: we are blocked, under the control of our blind spots, which lead us to make wrong deci-sions over and over again. *It's an inside job,* really.

I learned about blind spots and breakthroughs in the Land-mark Forum,[5] a course focusing on personal transformation and

---

5 Landmark Education (www.landmarkeducation.com), widely recognized as an industry leader for personal training and development, delivers programs and training that make a significant difference in those aspects of people's lives that they care about most.

living life fully. I had many personal breakthroughs from participating in the course. One of the main truths that surfaced was a blind spot related to my father, crucial information that, in turn, subconsciously affected all of my relationship choices.

After my parents divorced when I was twelve, I told a judge that I didn't want to see my father anymore. He granted me the right to make that decision. As a result of that decision, I didn't see my father for more than fifteen years. In fact, I later found out that for many years, my father didn't stop trying to see me.

When he would come for visitation, I hid; I didn't want to be found. Because of the dysfunction and the fighting and always being asked to take sides, I wanted to be far away from both of my parents. When I was still a child, I made the decision that I didn't need my father, and I acted as if and lived as though I didn't have one.

Fifteen years later, at the Landmark Forum, I had a breakthrough. I realized and immediately felt the impact of that decision I'd made, essentially "divorcing" my father. Not having him in my life was one of the reasons I'd been attracting inappropriate men *all those years*. I realized that the men I attracted were people I wanted to subconsciously "fix," so as to re-create my familiar, dysfunctional childhood.

I realized the actions I took as a hurt child would become some of the saddest of my life. I had a father, and I rejected him. In turn, I dragged that "story" around for years. Unbeknownst to me, it was my biggest blind spot.

Another important breakthrough had to do with my relationship to my family. As I mentioned, I had a rather lonely childhood. When I was born, my mother and her family stopped speaking over a disagreement that no one could remember. When I was nine, my mother and I ran into an old couple on the steps of the synagogue, and suddenly they all burst out crying. My mother then announced, "Bari, these are your grandparents." Ouch. I had grandparents and an aunt, uncle, and cousins I never knew about.

Because I didn't even know that I had any family until I was nine, all of my perceptions about my relatives came from my mother. Because of her childhood experiences, and never feeling like she fit in, her subtle and sometimes not-so-subtle messages conveyed that her family was all out for themselves. She thought her family didn't approve of my father as well as other misconceptions. My mother didn't get the love she needed, and she channeled all of that negative sentiment to me. And so it goes with the origins of our blind spots and the incidents in our lives to which we add meaning and take with us into adulthood.

After I completed the Landmark Forum, I realized immediately that I kept my cousins at a distance, even years later. On the one hand, I longed for closeness and love from them, especially having been an only child. On the other hand, despite this strong craving, I spent my life feeling that my cousins didn't really care about me. After the course, I called one cousin and made arrangements to see her. I told her about my breakthrough and how much I had always wanted to be closer to her. She replied that she always loved me, and that she too wanted to have a closer relationship. She told me that she would always be there for me. We both cried. At that moment, I really understood that it had been *me* that created and kept the distance between us. It was an amazing blind spot to have discovered!

After understanding the misguided relationship I had with my father, I immediately took action and contacted him. A few days later, I was on a flight from Florida to New York to see him. From the window of my cab, parked across the street from the Maimonides hospital in which I was born, I saw an adorable old man with red hair waiting to greet me. My stomach sank. *I'd missed so many years of his presence.*

At our reunion that day, he cried and shared his pain and sadness over those years of trying to find me. He felt such terrible rejection. After the divorce, he recounted how he went into a terrible depression, and for many years, he didn't want to live.

He asked so many questions about how it could have happened. How could such a decent guy deserve to be kicked out on the street with his possessions in garbage bags? I couldn't tell him why because I didn't understand it myself. After all, I was a child at the time, an innocent victim in this family. I sat and listened to his story, and told him how I regretted my own judgment, which led to the end of our relationship.

I spent two days in his world getting to know him again. He took me by the hand and we walked around his Boro Park neighborhood together. He showed me off to his friends. I realized from spending time with him that I got my creativity, sense of humor, and drive to search and seek from him.

This experience created a window for me to understand my parents. I was able to forgive them and to forgive myself. It was an incredible opportunity to help me move on. In the forum that I participated in through Landmark Education, I learned to be grateful to my parents simply for having given me life. Everything else beyond that was a bonus. I was able to relate to them in a new context, as people who did the best they could do for me at the time. *Breakthroughs allow for immediate action.* By discovering what lurks in the depths of yourself, you don't need to live another day stuck behind a blind spot.

Case Study: Susan, Age Thirty, on Fear

Susan, a thirty-year-old woman, began to tell me about her relationship goals and how she wants to find a long-term life partner. She added that all of her friends also want a *long-term relationship*, and that time is of the essence since they are all around thirty.

A long-term relationship? "Why not marry?" I asked. I remembered her saying how much she loves children and how often she finds herself playing with babies and children. I also remembered that she comes from a big family. "Do you want children?" I asked. She told me yes, she wants them, and that she loves children. I then asked her what her distinction is between wanting a long-term relationship and getting married. If she wants to find someone, create a long-term relationship, and create a family, why not commit? "What are you afraid of and what are your concerns?" She shrugged and said she wasn't sure. She would have to think about it.

Time and time again singles tell me that they want a long-term relationship, but they don't want to get married. When I ask them why, I typically hear completely illogical responses.

As I mentioned earlier, fear keeps us from having what we want. *Irrational fear.* What's the difference between rational fear and irrational fear? Rational fear comes from someone coming toward you with a knife or a wild animal about to attack you. But most of the time, since we're not living in the jungle or in a crime scene (hopefully), we're not dealing with sudden attacks. So the fear we suffer from is most often classified in the "irrational" category.

Susan clearly desires a connection, but *doesn't trust herself* to make a commitment or to find someone who will commit to her; she doesn't know that it's even possible. And if that is what she believes, it's likely that that is the direction her life will take—unless there is an interruption.

Where did the fear come from? Her generation, her belief systems, our society, the media, and the examples she's seen? Probably all of the above. Fear leads us to create *false* stories that we learn to believe about ourselves. These false stories keep us from finding the love we so desire, because they keep us from loving and connecting to ourselves. These stories keep us from being authentic. Being healthy and *loving ourselves* is the key to developing and sustaining a loving relationship.

Conquering Fear by Getting into Reality

To begin with a strong foundation today starts with stating your current reality so you can create your new future. An antidote to fear is getting into reality and challenging fear as invalid or irrational; it's just a feeling. People tend to draw conclusions about themselves that they think are true regardless of reality. These conclusions or "stories" can sometimes be very disempowering like, "There's something wrong with me," or "I'm not worthy," or "I don't deserve this." We usually create these stories as children and gather evidence to support the validity of stories as we get older.

The fact is that what appears to be real or true (like the stories we make up about ourselves) may not be true at all. For example, saying: "The dating scene is awful," or "All women are . . . ," or "All men are . . ." may not be true at all, even though there appears to be evidence. If we are going to assign meanings to events or stories about ourselves, let's create empowering ones.

Case Study: Mitch, Age Thirty-two

Mitch, a handsome, highly intelligent, sensitive man, came to me because he wanted to get married, and it was just not happening. Although he dates often, he keeps meeting women who seem very interested in him, but in reality they are "unavailable" and not ready to commit to marriage. During one of our dating for marriage coaching sessions, I asked Mitch the following questions:

Bari   How long have you been dating?

Mitch   More than ten years.

Bari   How long was your longest relationship?

Mitch   Six months.

Bari   How long have your parents been married?

Mitch   Thirty-seven years.

Bari   What are you looking for in a spouse?

Mitch   I want to be accepted, understood, and believed in, and I want to find someone who wants a family—the whole package.

Bari   What do you think your blockage related to dating has been?

Mitch   When I'm with a woman I'm interested in, or if I see a woman I like from a distance, I freeze up. It's hard to be myself. I feel and act like a person who does the opposite of what someone interested would do. I lose my confidence. If I'm with someone I'm not so interested in, it's not a problem, and most of my relationships have been with the wrong women who can't commit or aren't ready.

Bari   Why do you think you do those things?

Mitch   I become intimidated, like I have low self-esteem.

I continued asking him what deeper causes he thought might be behind the behavior. He thought for a while, and then said, "I think it's because it's risky and I would be vulnerable."

I wanted him to get to the core issue of what was behind "risky and vulnerable." I asked him, "What emotion does that conjure up? What drives you, really? Why are you intimidated, and what do you think is behind your lack of self-confidence?"

The answer he finally gave me, after thinking about it for a few moments, was in the form of a question. "Fear?" he replied.

"Yes, fear, definitely."

As we grow up, our personality development is shaped by our experiences. Since we're dependent on our parents and caregivers, much of who we are and who we become is already decided during a period of time we cannot even remember. According to the renowned psychologist Erik Erikson, our sense of trust (versus mistrust) and autonomy (versus shame and doubt) are ingrained in us by the age of three. As adults, we live with these personality traits, as if they cannot be changed. In fact, what we consider the truth about ourselves is not the truth.

Childhood and the Stories We Create

I harbored a delusion in the form of a story because of my childhood. It was as if I had written an unconscious sentence that "something is wrong with me" or, more generally, that "something is wrong." Because of this story, which I really believed, I ended up unconsciously attracting people who continued to make me feel that "something was wrong." It was my story, because my subconscious thoughts condemned me to a life of wrong relationships where I always felt unloved and misunderstood. I repeated this pattern without knowing why, until I interrupted it by becoming aware of this unconscious thinking.

Mitch, the man I was coaching, also made a decision about himself that was related to not wanting to be vulnerable and feeling intimidated by women he was interested in. The reasons we create these stories is less important than the impact they have on us. Their origins, however, are still worth exploring. I asked Mitch about his parents and childhood. Mitch's parents were married for thirty-seven years, and he described having had a happy childhood. His parents were intelligent and very engaged in science and engineering. His mother worked outside the home from the time he was little, and he and his sisters always had nannies.

What stood out for him as a child? He described the daily ritual of how he and his sisters would sit at the window waiting for their mother to come home. Mitch clearly remembered how joyful they were to hear the sound of her jingling the keys when she arrived. Could this be the source? Perhaps Mitch invented his "I am not worthy" story because his mother worked outside of the home. In his mind, had he been truly valued, maybe his mother would not have left him every day. This, at least, was the question on "Little Mitch's" mind.

The stories that we invent as children, which we hang onto later as adults, oftentimes keep us small and limited. We are not aware that they are controlling us. The older we get, the harder we grasp the stories, and the more closed off we become. The result: we stop putting ourselves out there. First, our mother or father "leaves" us; then we get laughed at in school; then we get rejected; and then and then and then . . . We stop taking risks. We decide that it's just too painful.

Have you ever noticed how children act? They spring out of bed at the crack of dawn and run around and splash in puddles with joy—and typically for no reason at all! Children declare happiness because "it's Thursday!" And adults? No way. So many adults become more and more bogged down, closed-off, tired, fearful, and cynical. After years of more and more pain, avoiding being hurt becomes the smart and sensible decision. By staying in the comfort zone, avoiding risk and failure, adults avoid exposing their sensitive underbelly. Although consciously they may know that vulnerability and risk are the only way to achieve worthwhile success, fear drives them to choose safety.

When we stop taking risks, we slowly lose our ability to experience joy in life, in all relationships, and especially in love. These are the unfortunate consequences of a story we make up about ourselves, a story that most likely isn't true. In believing that it is, though, we give the story power, and we gather evidence to support our lack of worth and deservedness of the negative experiences we endure.

> **Fact:** My parents had problems. They couldn't take care of me and they got divorced when I was twelve years old.
>
> **The story:** I convinced myself that these events meant that there was something very wrong with me. I convinced myself that I deserved the treatment I received. I convinced myself that I was damaged and was supposed to feel alone, period.

People add meaning to almost everything that happens in their lives. Through self-awareness and reflection people can achieve breakthroughs to unravel and separate the reality from the meaning of the story they created.

Mitch created the disempowering story that he was "unworthy," and therefore became intimidated by women he was interested in. The story dictated how he acted in life and how he related to women. As such, he only comfortably (unconsciously) attracted women who were not ready to get married or were emotionally unavailable. Until we began our work together, Mitch was unaware of his story and its implications, and he was definitely not free to be himself.

The Solution: Deconstruct, Invalidate, and Create an Empowering Story

In our sessions, I coached Mitch to challenge his negative, disempowering "story" and helped him to create a new, more empowering story to take its place. (See the Reality Check on page 74). Since Mitch was the one who created the disempowering story from his childhood, he had the ability within himself to create a new, more empowering story that relates to the man he is today. This positive, reality-based story would break the disempowering one that had been dragging him down for so long. His new empowering statement was:

I am a smart, warm, kind, generous, and spiritual man who deserves to be loved, accepted, understood, and believed in. I have a world of love to give, and I am ready to share my life, passions, and joy with a wife and soul mate. I am ready to build a life and create a family with my ideal spouse. I am ready to create our magnificent world together and share whatever life brings.

What Mitch said he wanted most in a relationship was to be accepted, understood, and believed in. I asked if he felt accepted, understood, and believed in as a child. He paused and said that he felt loved, yes, but since his parents were not demonstrably affectionate, he lacked the warmth of true acceptance.

It's no surprise that he attracted women who did not give him the acceptance, understanding, and affectionate love he needed. Mitch obviously didn't feel he deserved it. He was unaware that he was actually re-creating his childhood environment, the space where he was "comfortable."

By attracting the opposite of what he wanted, dating needy and unavailable women, he continued to reinforce the belief that he was unworthy. And feeling unworthy, he was socially uncomfortable going to venues where he might meet the "right" women. For years, he continued to attract the needy, noncommittal, unaffectionate women he felt he deserved. This was the energy he was putting out.

So, with his new awareness—his breakthrough—Mitch transformed his story into a more positive and powerful one. In the days and weeks that followed, he started to believe in himself. His life began to change. Newly empowered to take action, he learned to be comfortable in any situation. He'd faced his demons and slayed the dragon's voice inside of his head.

Mitch used various tools to support his new vision, and as a result, dramatically changed his life. He used visualizing techniques to fill in the My Happiness & Finding My Life Partner Journal (page 140) and to create a Meet to Marry Dream Board (page 156). He regularly focused his attention on his Dream Board and did daily journaling as tools to picture his new life clearly. He wrote down a date by which he wanted to be married in his journal, and he imagined how it would feel like to be with someone who met his needs (and he, hers). He got into action by filling out his Dating Plan of Action (page 202) and he began attending venues that previously made him feel uncomfortable. Despite his fear, he even became comfortable at singles events. Mitch was learning to lighten up and to finally be comfortable in his own skin. In time, he overcame the fear that sat on his shoulders, telling him he was not worthy. When his thoughts changed, his reality changed.

As human beings, we find meaning in, and create stories about, the events in our lives. As adults, we need to be introspective, willing to delve deep into ourselves in order to identify and reject these stories and disempowering belief systems that rob us of our ability to experience joy. Many of us, whether we're thirty, forty, or older than fifty, are walking around making decisions based on the belief system of a three-year-old child.

What's Your "Story"?

Beliefs have the power to create and the power to destroy.
Human beings have the awesome ability to take any

experience of their lives and create a meaning that disem-
powers them or one that can literally save their lives.

—Anthony Robbins

Here's a fact: We have what we have in our lives because that's how we set it up. *What we think about (even unconsciously) is what we attract into our lives.*

Think about your parents' relationship and what needs
  they met.
Think about the needs they didn't meet (or what you
  would have wanted).
Think about your first relationship, then the second,
  and all previous relationships.
Think about what you really want in a relationship.
Think about the things you want that you hold yourself
  back from.
Think about your blockages and your relationship patterns.

Here's another example of how you can uncover your own story using the Reality Check. I coached a woman I'll call Mary. Here are the questions I asked her and her responses:

Bari   How old are you?

Mary   Fifty-three years old.

Bari   How long was your longest relationship?

Mary   I was married for five years and I've been divorced for
         more than fifteen years now.

Bari   How long was your longest relationship since your divorce?

Mary   Oh, maybe six months. I haven't dated much since. I put my focus on raising my children.

Bari   What are your goals regarding marriage?

Mary   I am ready to get back into it; so I would say a year from now.

Bari   What are you looking for in a relationship?

Mary   I would like to have a wonderful, intimate marriage with someone I'm comfortable with, with no reservations. To experience travel and fun and someone who has good values like kindness, someone I can admire. I'd like to meet someone who has children and grandchildren . . . a loving guy.

Bari   How long were your parents been married?

Mary   Forty-three years [they are deceased].

Bari   What was your parents' relationship like?

Mary   My parents were great. They were married for a lifetime and had mutual respect for each other and really loved each other. My father was always there for my mom and she was there for him. They had the same values and they even took classes together; they were total partners. They raised a family. They never said unkind words to each other.

Bari   What needs did they meet?

Mary   They loved me and took care of me. I had a secure home life with a roof over my head and food to eat. They were

good role models and did their best to support me. I
knew they loved me.

Bari   What needs didn't they meet that you would have liked
from them?

Mary   I didn't get a strong feminine influence from my mom. She
was more in charge and my dad was more of the romantic. I don't feel like I was taught how to be a woman. I
was Daddy's little girl. I sometimes felt I was in competition with my mom because she was better at things than
I was. I wouldn't want to do things with her when I was a
girl because of that. Also, I had older male siblings, and
they were the ones who got great educations and more
advantages than I did because they were male. I think my
parents should have encouraged me the same way they
did the boys.

Bari   When you think about dating, how does it make you feel?

Mary   It feels a little overwhelming, the idea that I have to put
myself out there, and if someone isn't right for me it will
be difficult to swallow.

We continued our discussion and I asked her about her dating
life before marriage. She described attracting guys who weren't
serious or "guys who had girlfriends already and the guys would
just want sex and that was not for me. I wouldn't go for it; it was
a moral thing and they weren't really 'for' me."

Mary attracted guys who chose her and weren't available or
weren't interested in getting married, weren't educated, weren't

stable financially, and just wanted to have a good time, which left her feeling vulnerable. When I asked Mary why she married her husband, she said she basically wanted to get married; he came along, was the right religion, and was smart, and although he was limited emotionally and wasn't a passionate person, she married him. He chose her and she went along with it: "It was time to get married already."

I asked her what keeps her from having what she wants in a relationship. She replied that it's scary to put herself out there. Mary's emotional needs are to be cherished, loved, admired, and safe, as well as have humor, adventure, and passion. When Mary created her summary and read it out loud, here's how it came out:

> I am a fifty-three-year-old woman who was married for five years, and I have not dated much in the fifteen years since my divorce. My parents were loving toward each other and had respect for each other as they raised a family together. My parents met my needs by giving me a stable home life and roof over my head and did their best to educate me. What I would have liked to have had from them, my mother specifically, was more of a feminine role model to prepare me for the world and not to feel competition from her, and for them to have given me as many advantages as my brothers. I felt like I wasn't in the same league as them and that I was left on my own to make it in the world.

As her coach, it was clear to me what her story was, and I

wanted Mary to have a breakthrough. Mary is a loving and sup-portive woman, and a friend to all. She dedicates her life to help-ing others and raising her children. I thought, *Now that they are grown, it's her turn to find love.*

Back to the original question. What is Mary's "sentence" or "story" about herself? As I mentioned at the beginning, we have what we have because we have sentenced ourselves to something. When we are little children, we make up stories about ourselves (that are not necessarily true), and from these stories (from the mind of a little child), we subconsciously live life a certain way.

For Mary, when she was little, she felt in competition with her mom. She felt her brothers were more highly valued than she was and that they were encouraged more. She made a deci-sion about herself as a little girl. Her life revolved around that decision, and throughout her life, she gathered evidence that this sentence/story was true. But remember, it *wasn't* true. In reality, it was Mary's interpretation of certain events.

What was that outcome of her belief? Mary attracted guys who were unavailable and not smart, and then she settled for marrying someone who wasn't what she really wanted. Instead, she married someone who was very limited. Not surprisingly, it didn't work out.

She didn't get the education she wanted, but her brothers did.
Mary did not allow herself to be vulnerable.
Mary expressed fear.
Mary didn't put herself out there throughout her life.

Mary's pattern is to always be "good" and to help other
people.

Mary wants to be liked and accepted but doesn't trust herself.

I asked her if she agreed with this observation, and she did.

"What is the sentence you gave yourself for your life?" I asked.
"Why don't you step out? Why don't you allow yourself to be
vulnerable? What is your sentence?"

Eventually, she said, "I was fearful, and I guess I didn't really
allow myself to be vulnerable. Fear, right?"

"Yes, fear, but what's the sentence?"

After thinking for a few moments, she said, "I don't deserve it."

"Right! You don't deserve it. That's your sentence. So you
lived your life not deserving a great husband, not attracting men
who value you, because you didn't deserve it. You decided you're
not feminine enough or smart enough. And you gathered evidence of that. And because you made that decision so long ago,
you think it's true. And the craziest part is that this was all done
unconsciously. And guess what? We all do it!"

What I told Mary then, and what I'm here to tell you now, is
this: the great news is that now that you know your story is not
the truth, you can challenge it and create a new more empowering sentence or story about how amazing you are.

You get to create a new truth. You know that your parents
loved and adored you and you just added meaning to things that
happened. When you were a little girl, maybe you were playing a game with your mom and she won and you decided she's

competition. Who knows? But really, it doesn't matter. What does matter is that you are an adult and you are aware of your story.

You are aware of the fear, the deprivation, and the other behaviors that are "symptoms" of the story. Now you get to choose life powerfully and challenge your story and replace it with one that is reality-based and empowering!

Have a Breakthrough! Take the Reality Check

Discover how being unrealistic (or blocked) may be keeping you from finding the one! Establish your current reality by answering the questions on the following pages. Assess where you see yourself now and consider what, if any, blockages you may have that may be keeping you from your happiness. Discover what you may be telling yourself unconsciously and create your new empowering story!

Reality is a good thing. In fact, it's the only thing. If you get in touch with and become fully aware of your current reality, you can breathe easy and know that you are exactly where you need to be. How wonderful would it feel if you could let your guard down and simply allow life to unfold all of the time—even when dating to marry? That is precisely one of our goals.

1. How old are you?
2. How long have you been dating (or not dating)?
3. What are your goals for marriage? (i.e., when would you like to be married by?)
4. Why do you think it hasn't happened yet?
5. How long was your longest relationship?

6. How long have your parents been married? If divorced, for how long?

7. If your parents are/were divorced, how old were you when they got divorced?

8. What was/is your parents' relationship like? (i.e., my parents were close or fought all the time, or they adored each other, were affectionate and attentive, they were happy, etc.)

9. What needs of yours did your parents meet? (i.e., did you feel nurtured, did they listen to you, did they set a great example, give you a lot or little attention, make you feel loved, etc.)

10. What needs didn't your parents meet that you wish they had?

11. What do you think you want and need in a relationship? (i.e., someone caring, warm, and attentive, or someone who will be a generous, a great parent, etc.)

WHAT IS A BLOCKAGE?

A blockage is something that can keep you from having what you want. You may not realize that you have a blockage—also known as a blind spot—until it's brought to your awareness.

Blockages can come from external messages or stories we tell ourselves that may not be TRUE and we usually draw conclusions about ourselves from our childhood.

 EXAMPLES OF A BLOCKAGE:

BLOCKAGE: Someone who has been dating for more than ten years who believes "there is no one worth dating."

BLOCKAGE: Saying you want to get married, but not being in action about it or dating in all the "wrong" places.

BLOCKAGE: Limiting search criteria to either superficial elements (like looks or age) can limit the possibilities of great matches.

BLOCKAGE: Thinking that the answers are outside of yourself.

BLOCKAGE: Being closed-minded or negative.

12. What kind of people do you/or have you been dating/ attracting?

13. Do you see any patterns related to the kind of people you date?

14. How do you feel about dating? Are there things about dating you dislike?

15. What blockages do you think you may have, if any? (i.e., I have a fear of intimacy, or I don't date often, I feel insecure, which affects my dating, or I am intimidated easily, etc.)

16. What patterns have you noticed in various areas of your life, including your career, and life choices and dating?

17. Based on the needs you wish your parents could have fulfilled for you (whether real or not, true or not), what conclusions could you have come to about yourself?

18. Do you have a story (a belief system) about yourself that includes the phrases, "I don't deserve," "Something is wrong," "I'm not lovable," etc?

READER/CUSTOMER CARE SURVEY

We care about your opinions! Please take a moment to fill out our online Reader Survey at **http://survey.hcibooks.com.**

As a **"THANK YOU"** you will receive a **VALUABLE INSTANT COUPON** towards future book purchases

as well as a **SPECIAL GIFT** available only online! Or, you may mail this card back to us.

(PLEASE PRINT IN ALL CAPS)

First Name		MI.	Last Name	

Address				

State		Zip	Email	City

1. Gender
- ☐ Female   ☐ Male

2. Age
- ☐ 8 or younger
- ☐ 9-12   ☐ 13-16
- ☐ 17-20   ☐ 21-30
- ☐ 31+

3. Did you receive this book as a gift?
- ☐ Yes   ☐ No

4. Annual Household Income
- ☐ under $25,000
- ☐ $25,000 - $34,999
- ☐ $35,000 - $49,999
- ☐ $50,000 - $74,999
- ☐ over $75,000

5. What are the ages of the children living in your house?
- ☐ 0 - 14   ☐ 15+

6. Marital Status
- ☐ Single
- ☐ Married
- ☐ Divorced
- ☐ Widowed

7. How did you find out about the book?
(please choose one)
- ☐ Recommendation
- ☐ Store Display
- ☐ Online
- ☐ Catalog/Mailing
- ☐ Interview/Review

8. Where do you usually buy books?
(please choose one)
- ☐ Bookstore
- ☐ Online
- ☐ Book Club/Mail Order
- ☐ Price Club (Sam's Club, Costco's, etc.)
- ☐ Retail Store (Target, Wal-Mart, etc.)

9. What subject do you enjoy reading about the most?
(please choose one)
- ☐ Parenting/Family
- ☐ Relationships
- ☐ Recovery/Addictions
- ☐ Health/Nutrition
- ☐ Christianity
- ☐ Spirituality/Inspiration
- ☐ Business Self-help
- ☐ Women's Issues
- ☐ Sports

10. What attracts you most to a book?
(please choose one)
- ☐ Title
- ☐ Cover Design
- ☐ Author
- ☐ Content

FOLD HERE

Comments

Next, create a summary of your answers
and read it to yourself:

I am _____ years old and I have been dating (or haven't been dating) for _____ years.

My longest relationship was _____ (months/years).

I would like to be married by (or my plans for marriage are) _____
_____.

I think it hasn't happened yet because _____
_____.

My parents are/were married for _____ years. My parents' relationship is (was)_____
and because of that I _____
_____.

My parents met my needs by _____.

What I would have liked to have from them was _____
_____.

What I want most out of a relationship is (start with the words "to be" or "to feel") _____
and to find someone who _____
_____.

When I think about dating I feel _____
_____.

I may have a blockage in the following area_____
_____.

I notice the following relationship patterns and/or other patterns in my life _____

_____.

Based on the needs I wish my parents could have fulfilled for me (whether real or not, true or not), I may have drawn the following conclusions about myself _____

_____

_____

_____.

I may have a story or a belief system about myself that goes something like _____

_____

_____.

Now that you've completed the Reality Check, take a look at your answers and consider what you have written. What do you notice? Do you see any patterns related to the needs your parents didn't meet and the kind of people you attract and what you look for in relationships? Do you see any patterns related to your parents' relationship and how you are in relationships? Based on the reality of your dating history, are you ready to get into action and take positive steps toward achieving your dreams?

If you are present to your current reality, you can breathe easy and know that you are exactly where you need to be. This is a starting point for "being" the one.

Next, create a powerful vision of yourself and your future!

EXAMPLE: Someone who thought their parents paid more attention to a sibling (as in the example of Mary earlier in this chapter) may have felt "unlovable" or "unworthy" as a result, so their old story might be "I'm not lovable, otherwise my parents would have paid more attention to me." Right? Wrong! A child made that up. A new, more empowering reality-based statement for this person in the present based on their authentic self could be: "I'm a lovable, smart, sensitive, and generous person who is free and open to give and to welcome unconditional love in my life." Note: disempowering stories can influence your life choices and dating patterns and they are not based on a connection to your authentic self.

1. Look at your answer to question 18 from the Reality Check to review what disempowering story or belief system (if any) you may have about yourself and write it down in the "old story" column below. For example, "I don't deserve . . ." or "I'm not lovable . . ."

2. Next to it, replace that "old story" with one that is fact-based, empowering, and real (i.e., I am a sensitive, kind, and generous person).

➤ Old Story ➤

(i.e., Something is wrong with me. I am not worthy, desirable, or lovable.)

_____

_____

_____

_____

_____

_____

_____

➤ New Empowering Story ➤

(i.e., I am a generous, warm, and kind person ready to love someone and be loved.)

_____

_____

_____

_____

_____

_____

_____

It's never the "what happened" that is the problem, it's the meaning we add to the "what happened." To get to healthy thinking and into reality is to know that we're not doomed to live our lives dragging around the past and living "old stories." Rather we can choose to create new and empowered possibilities and live into any future that we invent for ourselves.

Reality—don't leave home without it.

Date to Marry Tip: Time is precious—don't
waste it being negative or in self-doubt.

There came a point when I was ready for a major shift in my life.
There was no turning back if I was to change and find the love and
life I truly wanted. I would cry about the time I'd wasted, how old I
was, and all the mistakes I'd made. I was clear that I didn't want to
be in the same place in one, three, or five years, and I was also clear
that there were two things I could count on—I was going to get older
and time was going to march on. If I was going to live my life, the
best choice was to live *powerfully. Time is the only thing you can't
get back, so get busy!*

I learned to transcend my situation and so can you. Part of
my journey was to learn to love myself with unconditional self-
acceptance. I shattered the story of my childhood by understanding that *where I landed was not my fault.* I was a baby then.
Today, as a grown woman, it's my responsibility to heal myself
and accept my past as where I came from and part of my journey. In the past, I saw myself as "flawed." Then I learned to work
with what I had, to continue perfecting God's creation, and to
see myself as lovable, just as I am.

I achieved this by recognizing the need to get off of my own
back. I started to view myself more tenderly, with forgiveness
and compassion. If I reject myself, then surely others will, too.
On the other hand, if I accept and love myself with an innocence

born of no judgment of the past, I'll draw like-minded people to me, heart and soul.

In the past, the men I attracted were men who were not a reflection of my true essence. They were the by-product of how I felt about myself. Correspondingly, they gave little because I didn't feel worthy. As I grew in self-awareness and self-love, I eventually attracted Michael, a man who is generous, giving, and open, a life partner reflecting my "polished mirror." Become your own polished mirror by learning to accept yourself. To increase your self-acceptance:

- Don't judge yourself—you can't change your past actions, but you can change your future.
- Don't criticize yourself—give yourself a break!
- Don't use "shoulds," "coulds," and "maybes"—you're right where you're supposed to be.
- Do make a list of *everything* you have to be grateful for, including the lessons you've learned along the way.

4

Moving Beyond the Fear

Courage is resistance to fear, mastery
of fear—not absence of fear.

—Mark Twain

Fear (f. e. a. r.) is false evidence
appearing real.

—Alcoholics Anonymous

Fear manifests itself in our lives in many ways. It creates blockages in our energy and clouds our self-image: who we want in our lives and the direction we want to be heading. However, when you reflect objectively on your own "fear patterns," you'll begin to see that we always attract what we are ready for and what we feel we deserve. Many singles sabotage their future in a variety of ways:

- *Not "living in reality."* Example: a forty-eight-year-old bachelor who has been limiting his search to twenty-five-year-olds. Another example: single women in their late thirties who only want to date men who were never married and without children, or with certain interests, careers, or income levels. By looking for someone half his age, what is the forty-eight-year-old really looking for? Does he really want a life partner or someone who will look good on his arm and validate him? If you are in your thirties or forties, you are likely to meet divorced men with children; by eliminating them, you would be eliminating a large pool of potentially matching men. A healthy, realistic way to view this particular situation is to see that family can happen in many ways and that divorced men have relationship experience and their own unique journey.
- *Carrying around negative associations related to dating.* Example: a single thirty-year-old woman who has been dating for ten years says she hates dating and everything about it, describing it as painful. Or someone who deep down really wants to get married but outwardly projects emphasis on career.
- *Not taking action consistent with achieving the dream.* Example: someone who states their desire to get married

as soon as possible, but doesn't date or limits the types of activities he/she is willing to participate in (singles' events or other social groups).

- *Not being true to yourself and abandoning your needs.* Example: living with a significant other, often for years, when you really want to be married or wanting a deep emotional connection but only seeking outward qualities.
- *Being overly critical and/or cynical about yourself and dating.* How can you expect to get from others what you won't give to yourself? Unconditional self-acceptance is the key to having love in your life. By being overly critical or cynical, you are not being an open channel for giving and receiving and you could actually be repelling what you want the most. Human essence is not analytical and critical, but rather open and connected.
- *Going to all the "right places" but not "being accessible."* Example: Singles "doing" all the right things (like focusing on outward appearance, networking, being active on dating sites, etc.), but a conversation with them reveals they are hardened, cynical, and closed.

. . . and the list goes on. Sound familiar? How about these beliefs:

- Dating for many years and no one is ever right.
- Repeatedly attracting the wrong people.
- Feeling you are not lovable.
- Feeling that no one can measure up to your expectations.

Fact: the past does not equal the future

Fear is a pervasive problem in the singles community. Taking their past experiences as rock-solid evidence of their "dating ineptitude," singles don't trust themselves and their judgment about dating and whom to date. Many singles report they are always wondering if someone better will come along (even when they are on a date). Masking their fear and insecurity is the tendency to blame perceived external circumstances: "Where are all the available men and women?" some may ask. The answer: They were there the whole time. You weren't able to recognize them (or attract them), because your blind spots, fears, and stories clouded your vision and obstructed your judgment. The growing nature of fear causes many people's situations to become more desperate over time. Unless people make changes in themselves as they get older and spend more time in "the scene," their levels of cynicism, confusion, and disillusionment only increase.

Slogan: "Reality—Don't Leave Home Without It!"

This became my mantra. This was so important, because in actuality, I lived my life with a very warped sense of reality. I went against the flow of life, and in order to go with the flow of life, I needed to be more authentic and true.

It wasn't a new message. One thing I knew about myself was that my best quality was my ability to see the best in people and that my worst quality was my ability to see the best in people. I wasn't a good judge because I couldn't see what was real—seeing only the good I couldn't differentiate between what was and what wasn't healthy. Seeing only the good, I operated in fantasy mode in all of my relationships. It was nearly impossible for me to identify and express what I needed. Convinced of the "something is wrong with me" story, I attracted men who could never meet my needs: they were typically emotionally immature, narcissistic, or unavailable.

From Fakakta to Reality: A Step-by-Step Approach

*Fakakta: a word of Yiddish origin, used
to describe something that doesn't work well, or
a person or thing that is completely crazy.*

In the past, my thinking was fakakta: the total picture I had of myself, dating, and marriage was unhealthy, to say the least. I needed to stop thinking so much and just "be." With this insight, it became clear how much I focused on the negative and on the future, making it impossible to begin to live in the moment. Allowing life just unfold was not in my vocabulary. However, I learned to challenge my unhealthy thinking patterns and replace them with more empowering and positive messages.

I began to uncover my blind spots. I started to treat myself with compassion, and to forgive and to be a mother to myself. Without doing so, how could I expect to get from someone else that which I wouldn't give to myself? I began to honor the fact that I'm part of nature, and that where I landed as a child was not my fault. I had done my best, and it was high time that I got off my own back.

Really breaking through requires a commitment to identifying your blocked thinking and dysfunctional behavior patterns. *Breaking through also requires the readiness to make changes that are sometimes painful yet necessary for growth.* The rewards for reaching this difficult place are well worth your effort: *you finally get to have what you want.*

The Buddhist concept "wherever you go, there you are," sums up the message I want to impart to you: whether you're in L.A., Miami, rural Canada, Outer Mongolia, or Timbuktu, *it all begins with you.* Step back far enough for a truly objective view of the world. We are all adults with wounded children inside, children who need and deserve our attention. This is your opportunity, right now, to seize this chance for love. With a new view of yourself, you can uncover your blind spots, have breakthroughs, and reach a place where finding real love is not only possible, it's a certainty.

You are lovable and deserve to find the love you want. The key to finding love is first to love and accept yourself unconditionally, and to see yourself with compassion and without harsh judgment. *You* have to be "the one."

The process begins with assessing yourself for marriage readiness: identifying your blind spots, your blockages about yourself, and your attitudes toward dating. Taking a clear, objective look at "the man/woman in the mirror" will allow you to reframe any unhealthy images you may have about yourself. This work is necessary to continue in this process.

Simply put, identifying problem areas and assessing them leads to defining specific solutions to your specific deficiencies. This may involve encouraging exercises in self-empowering behavior, altering negative thinking patterns to positive ones, or increasing your self-esteem.

Analysis of the patterns in past relationships will enable you to reach the path of self-love, self-acceptance, and finally self-promoting behaviors and values, which are so critical for entering into a healthy relationship. When we are visible to ourselves, we can be visible to others. What are your behaviors or thought patterns that keep you from really loving yourself? What are your negative stories? By examining thoughts and behavior patterns objectively, it's possible to change attitudes and "reframe" behavior in the present. You can gain clarity about how you may unconsciously be sabotaging yourself. You can choose your thoughts and your moods.

Science, specifically the field of psychoneuroimmunology, is now supporting the idea that we *can* choose our thoughts and attitudes—as human beings, we are not limited by our genetics. Emotional intelligence[6] can be cultivated and learned at any stage in life. Choose to be happy and choose positive thoughts and create a positive experience. Psychologist Martin Seligman

---

6 Goleman, Daniel. *Emotional Intelligence*. Bantan, 1997. Emotional intelligence (EI) is a self-perceived ability to identify, assess, and control the emotions of oneself, of others, and of groups.

points out that "moods like anxiety, sadness, and anger don't just descend on you without your having any control over them . . . you can change the way you feel by what you think."

Is remaining in the dark about your blind spots worth sacrificing your humanity and your dreams? Of course not! Just ask yourself who you want be when it comes to finding love and you'll find the courage to explore.

Don't Listen to Really Bad, Well-Intentioned Advice

As well-meaning as friends and family can be, you've probably received your share of misguided advice. Women are often told to "calm down" and not worry about the time, as if any hint of marriage-mindedness would ward off men like the plague. Most important, you may have been vehemently warned: "Don't tell him [or her] you want to get married! You'll scare him [or her] off!" The confusion generated by this kind of advice can leave you in an even more panicked state. Many "experts" giving advice are not even married themselves. My advice is: don't listen. Make healthy choices for yourself.

Really Bad Advice

A thirty-three-year-old woman shared with me what she was told when she consulted a male dating coach. Concerned about her time clock, she was looking for some real advice. She didn't want to waste time dating men who might not be interested in marriage and children; she was thirty-three, and fertility-related issues could become a problem in a few more years. Unfortunately, she received advice that was disappointing. Rather than encouraging her to be true to herself, the coach advised her to simply manage her anxiety and not reveal "too early on" that she was marriage-minded or risk scaring guys off.

Here's what Karen shared with me about her encounter with him:

I told the coach that I'm thirty-three and I'm having a very difficult time finding "the one" now. I further told him that honestly, I didn't give it priority until the last few years and that when dating, there's no way to know if a guy is interested in marriage and children.

In my twenties, I was very carefree about dating, living together, travelling together—just having fun, and I didn't even think much about the future—there was plenty of time. Now it feels as though my clock is running out, and I'm worried because I just broke up with my boyfriend because after two years he told me I wasn't the one. So if I do this again and date someone for two or three years, I'll be over thirty-five, and I don't have time to waste.

I asked the coach how long he recommended dating before bringing up the ever-important question, "Where is this relationship headed?"

He advised her to just relax and not let her emotions or her anxiety get the best of her, not to worry about her biological clock, and to just give it time to see if a guy comes around. He suggested that even bringing up the idea of marriage too soon would scare off the average guy.

Karen: He told me to just chill out and don't allow the situation to overwhelm me. Go with the flow and enjoy the moments! Men don't like it when women share their desires too early on—it makes them uncomfortable. He said that if I look at a man like a future husband, he will run the other way, and that while it seems like sharing my marriage goals up front with the guy is the right thing to do, it's a mistake. He told me that I need to play by the rules and that when a guy falls for me he'll come around and get committed.

He further told her to just lighten up and that she should take up yoga or meditation instead of feeling anxious. He told her to be light and open when she dates and not to offer it up too quickly or she'll eliminate any possibility with men before it even happens.

Karen: He said that if a man is interested in having a future with me, I'll know; but it has to be his idea. He said I should just have a good time and relax and let nature take its course.

Our conversation continued:

Bari: The advice he gave you comes from his own personal point of reference, which conveys that *all* men have a fear of commitment. All men are not like him, and unfortunately, that type of advice is all too common and not the least bit empowering. Many men are marriage-minded and interested in marriage as much as you are.

I'd like to validate and support you and your intelligent dating instincts. I salute you for asking difficult questions and for being ready to move to the next stage of your life. The most important bit of wisdom I can share with you is to trust your instincts. Take charge of your destiny and your future by *being* someone who is marriage-ready.

I recommend that you develop a clear vision of yourself, your life, your values, and the future you desire to attract the right person into your life. It's important to seek out and attract like-minded men who share a common vision of marriage. As it stands now, you are attracting and meeting "mystery men" whose life goals are unknown, making dating seem random. Keep in mind that the amount of time you date someone is not what's important; rather, it's the quality of time spent having meaningful conversations and discussing core values and goals.

Again, having difficulty finding the "right one" is not just an issue that women face. There are just as many men wondering where the marriage-minded women are. Fear, or fear of commitment, comes up for people when they don't trust their own ability to be fully present in a relationship and they are not conducting themselves like marriage-minded individuals. They may not have a clear vision of their future and their emotional needs; they may carry around baggage from the past and are terrified of losing independence or being controlled. The irony is that it's actually in the context of a relationship where the deepest of connections exist, when we allow ourselves to be fully present, generous, and open to each other. When you conduct yourself like a marriage-minded, confident woman, your experience of dating will change. Don't hide the best of who you are. Don't buy into the "play the game" and "chill out" advice. It's definitely not timely or true. Share proudly who you are, what makes you tick, and, among other things, that what makes you special and unique is that one of your life goals is to get married and have a family. Time is something you cannot get back, and in my opinion, you are correct in not wanting to waste time with the wrong people. I congratulate you and wish you success on your journey.

This kind of advice is representative of the need for the paradigm shift, the need for you to live your life powerfully, articulate your goals, and change your world.

> *He says: You can't be too serious. . . .*

I say: Yes, you should be serious about your life goals and your future, because it is your life, so live it with passion, clarity and ease.

> *He says: The more you consider each man as a potential husband, the more each man is going to run the other way.*

I say: Do view each person you date as a potential spouse and the mother or father of your children and talk to each other. If they are not suitable candidates, find ones who share your vision and who inspire you.

> *He says: Chilling out and giving it whatever time it takes is the way to go.*

I say: Don't play games with your life. Self-love, communication, and knowing what you want and need in a relationship—that's still your "soundest bet." When it's right, you'll both be on the same page.

> *He says: By sharing your intentions up front, you're actually turning men off.*

I say: Speaking from the heart and being clear about who you are and what you want for yourself is empowering. Self-sabotage would be to waste time with someone who doesn't share your vision or wasting time "wishing and hoping" that someone will change.

He says: Men are immature and the idea of commitment needs to come from them so it's really important to let him feel he's in charge and have it be his idea. Win him over first, and if it's right, you're in a much better position to get him to commit.

I say: The game-playing and manipulation he suggests are not healthy ways to go, and won't work for the long-term.

There's no shortage of disempowering and "follow the rules" advice. *Reject the bad, disempowering advice and choose a paradigm shift.* My goal is to challenge and empower you to make new choices for yourself and your future by approaching dating in a whole new way. The negative, quick-fix, disempowering rhetoric is typical from "normal," well-meaning people. Choose to reject it, though, and create any outcome you want.

Dating Myths and Stereotypes

Dating Myth #1: Men Are the Problem[7]

---

7 There is a stereotype that men corner the market on commitment problems, and I wish to dispel this notion. In my encounters with singles, the stereotype exists in both genders, but women are more vocal about the problem than men. Throughout the book, I share the stories and triumphs of both genders in the hope of dispelling the myth. Since men and women are both of the human species, they both seek connection, but because of the current paradigm, they are not connecting or they are connecting with inappropriate matches.

Women love to call men "commitment-phobic." The vast majority of "dating" literature out there today addresses how to conquer men. It's common to see advice for "smart, successful, and powerful women" or "how to get a man, land a man, seduce a man, and get a man to want you."

Most dating and relationship books are written for women. Men, unlike women, do not sit around discussing their feelings and dating woes over a beer. It's not their style or in their nature to analyze their love lives the way women do. Men are just not like the girls in *Sex and the City,* supporting one another while figuring it all out.

What women can analyze for days ("Why didn't he call?" or "What does it mean that he didn't call me?"), men couldn't care less about. We often laugh about the fact that women have a hundred buttons of emotional complexity, while men have an on-and-off switch. What we miss in this mess is this: *men also want to make meaningful connections.* My coaching and conversations with men reveal the same concerns that women have. Where are the marriage-minded women? They share with me their dating woes and how difficult it is to make a real connection. Men as well as women are not conducting themselves like marriage-ready, confident individuals, so often they attract the exact opposite women from what they need.

Again, if you are not meeting and attracting the kind of man or woman you are looking for, here's a radical idea—the answers are not "out there." Instead, it's all about *you* and the kind of people and the mode of dating you have subscribed to.

Now, you may be thinking this notion doesn't work because it seems to be true for everyone you know, but that is herd-mentality thinking. Again, your life is in your hands! In the chapters that follow, you will read about dating for marriage, a powerful new way to date with clarity and empowerment.

Dating Myth #2: You Are Confused Because Your Parents Are Divorced

I always thought that the only confused singles were the product of dysfunctional childhoods or divorced parents, much like mine. But contrary to that, through all my research and years of experience, I have found that the blockages are not limited to those whose childhoods were less than ideal. Singles who grew up in intact homes with parents who set positive examples suffer from the same confusion and paralysis when it comes to dating. The reasons I hear include "I'll never meet someone as great as my dad" and "No one out there is good enough." I coached a forty-two-year-old woman whose parents were married for forty-six years who described her childhood as enchanting. Her parents were great partners and she has wonderful family memories, but she remembers feeling or hearing that she was spoiled. She told me that her mother was extraordinarily supportive of her, always providing encouragement and positivity, but as a young girl (because *she* decided she was spoiled) she felt was underdeserving of her mother's love and support. She chose instead to accept the more critical tone her father provided: "You're not going out dressed like that, are you?" So at forty-two, after two divorces from spouses who cheated on her and various financial struggles, her story about herself was that she was undeserving in her relationships and financial life; she doesn't deserve to have a trusting spouse, she doesn't deserve financial stability (having chosen a career as a social worker), and so on. This breakthrough set her free! The "stories" we invent are pervasive and are not limited to children of divorce and dysfunction. You can create your powerful future based on reality and create clarity for yourself to design the life of your dreams.

If You *Really* Want to Get Married, Don't Live Together

Recently, a woman shared her story with me: it was clear she was looking for answers. She told me that she had been living with her boyfriend for four years and that she was "happy" except that she really wanted to get married. She felt quite intertwined with him: they had a joint bank account and lived in a one-bedroom apartment. Her boyfriend was happy with the situation as it was. Her concern was that he had recently decided to focus all his efforts on his music career, when all the while she had been telling him for years that she wanted to get married. He kept telling her that he wasn't ready.

The lifestyle of a traveling musician in a band wouldn't work well with her life vision of marriage and children. He told her he wasn't ready for that conversation or the commitment she wanted. Although he told her he "wasn't ready," he made her an alternative suggestion. Since real-estate prices had tumbled, he proposed that they should buy a house together.

What makes seemingly intelligent people sacrifice their dreams? Fear: *f*alse *e*vidence *a*ppearing *r*eal. She decided, yet again, to give him six more months to see what would happen. She thought that he would change by then or she would make him leave. I asked why she was waiting. Of course, she had her reasons: he doesn't have anything, it's my furniture in the apartment, and so on. She didn't understand that *time is precious and you can't get it back*.

Sadly, the months became years, and before she knew it, she had sold out herself *and* her dreams for someone else's clock, hoping that he'd change. Again, reality: don't leave home without it.

Rabbi Shmuley Boteach, author of *Kosher Sex,* says that the best gift a man can give a woman is for him to ask her to marry him. When a man says that he is not ready to marry at this time, the answer is not that he is not ready to get married at this time, but rather, *he's just not ready to marry you.* Her boyfriend was actually honest and straightforward about his position. His actions supported his position. The question remained with her: *Is having "almost what you want" better than having no love at all?* Why should her boyfriend commit? He's happy with the current situation. His needs are being met, and he has the illusion of freedom while receiving the comforts of a spouse. They danced around the issue. She allowed her fear to paralyze her thinking and actions, sacrificing her needs and her dreams simply to be with someone. She feared being alone, so she did nothing, clinging to the hope that it would change.

Mariah Wojdacz of LegalZoom.com, a leading online legal service center, writes: "The highest risk factor for divorce may be surprising, since living together is often seen as a way to promote stability and security in a relationship. Couples who move in together prior to marriage have a far greater chance of divorce than couples who do not. How much higher is that risk? Some studies suggest couples who cohabitate before marriage, divorce at a rate as high as 85 percent."[8]

We can all learn something from this very common situation. Looking fear in the face allows us to conquer it, to be in reality, to go for our dreams. The moral of this cautionary tale? If you *really* want to get married, *don't* live together! *Time is the only thing you can't get back.* It's your life that's at stake!

---

8 http://www.chabad.org/library/article_cdo/aid/448427/jewish/Dating-the-Jewish-Way.htm

Case Study: Nina, Age Twenty-Four, Uncovers a Major Blockage

Smart, pretty, and very resourceful, Nina has been dating for marriage for years. Even at her age, her relationship history has been complex. At eighteen, she lived with an abusive boyfriend for a year and a half, and only escaped from the relationship with the help of a good friend. Without this friend, she may very well have had "cement shoes" for years.

Her next relationship, at age twenty-one, was with a man she met on a dating site. She ended up living with him for about a year. Interested mainly in football and home-improvement projects, he couldn't meet her emotional needs, and he didn't pay much attention to her. He seemed happy to have Nina as a live-in girlfriend, cook, and buddy to hang out with. Since he wasn't "in love" with her, they eventually stopped sleeping together, and they soon decided to break up.

At twenty-three, she got together with an old flame named Matt, whom she'd met many years earlier before her first relationship. Matt was recently divorced and Nina was suddenly "available," so the reconnection seemed to come at the "right time." At the time, Matt was in the military, stationed overseas with three years of military service remaining. They were both very excited about their new relationship, and she flew to a base in Europe to see him for a reunion. As so many years had gone by since first having met, it was a magical four-day experience, and he proposed quickly. Back at home and in the midst of wedding plans,

Nina got nervous, felt that that she'd made a big mistake, and called off the engagement. She realized that Matt wasn't the one: she didn't want to be a military wife and live overseas, and he was really only right for her on paper; she didn't feel it. Although he was a big improvement over her other boyfriends (he would have been there for her emotionally), she felt in her gut that if she married someone who was not right for her, that it would only end with heartache and pain later on.

It was at this point that Nina came to me for dating-for-marriage coaching. She wanted to break her patterns and understand why, at twenty-four, she was attracting the wrong people. She was perplexed that at her age, she already had a long dating history.

We began the coaching process by completing the Reality Check (see page 74), which helped her get in touch with her situation and become ready to make some changes in her life. We discussed her behavior patterns and the choices she made when dating and how those choices were actually tied to her past. She got in touch with her goals, dreams, emotional needs, and important values.

We worked together to create her vision of marriage by using the Marriage Vision forms to articulate her emotional needs (My Top 5 Emotional Needs, page 165), her values (My Values Worksheet, page 169), and her life goals (Life Goals Exercise, page 174). Over the weeks that followed, she began to respect and honor her emotional needs and was able to articulate them. With her new ability to identify suitable and available marriage-minded men, Nina was ready to jump into dating-for-marriage action.

Eventually, Nina met Josh on another dating site. Since Josh lived in New York and Nina was in Atlanta, they spoke regularly on the phone for several weeks, logging many hours of conversation before they decided to meet in person. She preferred to meet him on his turf, so she flew to New York and stayed in a hotel nearby. Josh met her at the hotel, and they enjoyed a dinner filled with wonderful conversation. According to Nina, everything flowed beautifully. He was very open with her, saying he wanted to find his best friend and life partner, and he was willing to relocate for the right person. They had the same vision of marriage, family, spirituality, and the logistics of living together. They simply clicked.

Everything progressed smoothly, until after the date when he escorted her to her hotel room, and he gently came close to kiss her. She felt nothing. No chemistry at all. Worst of all, she found herself turned off and upset. At that point, Nina suggested that he leave. She felt confusion, fear, and panic and was genuinely upset. Here is an excerpt from our session the next morning:

Bari: What happened?

Nina: I wanted to run and go home. Had he come to see me in Atlanta, I would have made him leave and would have asked him never to contact me again. It freaked me out.

Bari: It's a little familiar, isn't it?

Nina: Yes, I guess.

Bari: Let's get to the root of it. Let's talk about your parents. What are your emotional needs?

Nina: To be loved, appreciated, and . . . have a lot of attention and partnership.

Bari: What do you remember about your parents' relationship?

Nina: Basically, my dad was very affectionate and needed affection, but my mom would always push him away. There was very little if any love between them, and as a child, I could see it. It was so sad. I remember how much I loved my dad and how I would fall asleep on his chest, listening to his heartbeat. Mom was always very cold to him—like my grandmother was cold toward my grandpa. Grandpa was really a mush too. They were all very affectionate toward my brother and me, just not to each other.

Bari: Do you hear how you just described your parents' relationship? You desperately wanted love and affection, but you couldn't have it, because it wasn't comfortable. Now you still reject that which you want so much. You have taken on your mom's role and her feelings.

Nina: Oh my gosh! Wow! I see that. I never saw that before.

Bari: It's what you saw and experienced growing up: intimacy is wrong and not natural. Do you see? You are taking on your mom's fear of intimacy. It's not the guy and the kiss, is it?

Nina: No, it's not. I'm being just like my mom—and my grandmother. I can't believe it! I never saw that before.

Bari: Right, that's what we do. We are attracted to and we mimic our parents—both their positive and negative traits. You handle intimacy like your mom because it's what you saw. You don't feel like you deserve the love. You want it, of course, but it's foreign. To you, intimacy is bad.

Nina: That's crazy! I just realized, too, that when there is nothing at stake, when the guy is not able to commit, or when there's obviously no future with him, I don't have those feelings of wanting to run.

Nina continued to explain that her parents divorced while she was still a child, and shortly after both her parents remarried; she never saw the love and affection in either marriage that she envisioned for her own marriage.

Bari: Nina, with your new awareness, how do you feel?

Nina: This is an amazing breakthrough—I never put two and two together before. But I *am* uncomfortable about intimacy, especially public displays of affection. I'm really uneasy when I see people cuddling and snuggling. How do I get over that?

Bari: Now that you're aware of this, you can own it. Instead of running from this guy, you've got to communicate with him. If he's the right one, it will be safe to share your feelings about who you are, how you grew up, and how this affected what happened last night between you. If he's the right one, he'll understand that it wasn't him, and it wasn't the kiss. But you were able to get to the bottom of your fear of intimacy. This is a huge blockage for you, and you've broken apart the story you built about it. The awareness will allow you to challenge and overcome it.

Nina: Yes. I'm going to talk with him and tell him about my breakthrough.

Bari: Now that you know, you can confront the fear, challenge it, and walk through it. I can promise you that the fear will accompany you. It will sit on your right shoulder, and it will tell you that you don't deserve love. It will keep telling you that intimacy is scary. With courage, you've got it in you to feel the fear and do it anyway. You can challenge those thoughts and know they are invalid. Remember, fear is "false evidence appearing real." Let's do the Challenge Your Thinking exercise.

Nina: All right.

Bari: A: Identify the event that caused the upset.

Nina: Josh kissed me, but it didn't feel right at all. I freaked out, and I wanted to run and close off completely.

Bari: B: What did you feel? What were the emotions?

Nina: Confusion, fear, panic—I was upset. I just wanted to get as far away as possible.

Bari: C: What did you tell yourself? What was the automatic thought?

Nina: How could I have so much in common with someone and feel attracted to him, but when we kiss, there's nothing there? What is going on? This is so scary, confusing, painful, upsetting, and I want to run. Full-out panic. Something is wrong with me, and I'm not attracted to him. I can't be with him, this is crazy. How could this happen?

Bari: D: Great, but what is the rational response about the actual situation with Josh? What is the reality of Josh and the situation?

Nina: He's a great guy who I've been speaking with for weeks. He's caring and interested in pursuing a discussion of marriage with me. He is mature and open, and he's only displayed caring and compassion toward me. He's respectful. We have common goals and the same vision of the future. He's attractive, and we enjoyed spending time with each other.

Bari: E: How do you feel now?

Nina: I see that I need to look at my own fears, and I see that they aren't real or rational.

Bari: Right! The reality hasn't changed. You just dismantled what happened. You looked at your reaction rationally. By recognizing that, you can move ahead. You can challenge your thinking and act accordingly.

In the end, Nina spoke with Josh, and he was compassionate and understanding. Nina spent the next day with him and she realized that he was not the one for her. This time, she came to the conclusion rationally, not with the same old reactive, fearful reasoning. Something was just missing.

When Nina told Josh that she didn't want to continue the relationship, he appreciated her honesty. He wished her only happiness, and she wished the same for him. Armed with a new attitude and confidence, Nina went back to Atlanta and continued to go on coffee dates but wasn't meeting anyone matching.

Exactly two weeks later, Nina was introduced to a guy by a close friend who knew them both, and after doing some research about each other, they spoke on the phone. This began the six-hour-long conversation that would forever change her life. After their second phone conversation a few days later, he asked when they could meet in person. From the way he communicated with her and shared himself and what he was about, she was inspired by him and she knew he was a *very* special guy; different from anyone she'd ever met (after a long dating history for both of them). Two days later they met in person, and on their first date, she knew he was the one. Three months later, right before New Year's they were married and now live happily building their lives in marriage bliss. *When it's right, it will flow.*

Have a Breakthrough:
Do the Challenge Your Thinking Exercise

Take charge of your thoughts and future! Feelings aren't facts. Facts are facts!

The exercise will challenge your old way of thinking and empower you for the future. Use the exercise below to work through either an upsetting scenario or a situation where your thinking is negative or fixed and replace it with a healthier, more balanced and peaceful state of mind. You'll have the opportunity to see and apply realistic and reality-based thinking to any upsetting situation. It's time to break up disempowering thinking. Getting upset about events or circumstances is not about "what happened" but the meaning we add to "what happened."[9]

Example: "Joanna still hasn't returned my call since I called her after our date two nights ago." One way to think about this is to obsess and feel upset that she hasn't called. Another way is to interrupt this thinking process and say: "Wait! Even if she doesn't call me, it doesn't mean I'm not a desirable person! She may just be busy, or not a match. And if we are not matched, it will free me up to meet someone who is." You can control your thoughts and your destiny and come from a place of power in your life. Let's begin. Think of a situation that is upsetting or annoying, or a persistent complaint.

A. What is happening? Describe the circumstances or an event leading to an unpleasant emotion related to dating you have experienced in the past or are experiencing now that is upsetting, annoying, or a persistent complaint. EXAMPLE: The people I date talk only about themselves! They don't ask questions about me. _____

_____

_____

B. What are you telling yourself about the above circumstances? EXAMPLE: I tell myself that I'm not interesting or not good enough (or they would ask and be interested). Something must be wrong with me._____

_____

_____

9 Based on Rational Emotive Behavior Therapy (REBT), a psychotherapeutic system of theory and practices and a school of thought established by Albert Ellis, Ph.D.

C. How are you feeling as a result of the situation? Write down your emotions and behavior as a result of the event. EXAMPLE: Depressed, lonely, despondent, and turned off to dating. _____

_____

_____

_____

_____

_____

D. Challenge your answer to B with something more rational and empowering. EXAMPLE: It's not about me. If a person is self-absorbed, not asking questions, and talking only about himself or herself, I should not waste my time with him or her. I am lovable and smart. I will begin to love and trust myself and not surrender my power to others. _____

_____

_____

_____

_____

_____

E. How do you feel now that you've replaced irrational thoughts with rational ones? EXAMPLE: Hopeful and balanced. I realize that I can choose who to date and who to allow into my world. I will continue to develop myself and have a positive attitude and see myself in a new way every day. _____

_____

_____

_____

_____

_____

Date to Marry Tip: Be marriage-ready, available, and healthy.

When I was dating for marriage, I became happy, and for the first time I was really standing on my own two feet emotionally. I made a decision to change, and I did. I was busy going out and taking care of myself; I was dating and traveling as part of my healthy life.

Live your life! Be as happy, healthy, and complete as you can be in your own interests and expressed values. While this might seem obvious, it's good to keep in mind, since many of us have a long dating history or are learning to date consistent with our vision and taking this on in a whole new way.

Part II

ATTRACT
Your Ideal Spouse: Principle-Based Dating

The program is comprised of three parts: Assess—Attract—Act to get you "being" the one and fully ready and engaged in dating for marriage.

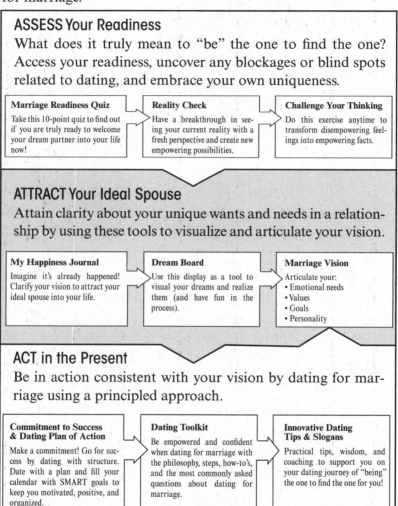

ASSESS Your Readiness
What does it truly mean to "be" the one to find the one? Access your readiness, uncover any blockages or blind spots related to dating, and embrace your own uniqueness.

Marriage Readiness Quiz
Take this 10-point quiz to find out if you are truly ready to welcome your dream partner into your life now!

Reality Check
Have a breakthrough in seeing your current reality with a fresh perspective and create new empowering possibilities.

Challenge Your Thinking
Do this exercise anytime to transform disempowering feelings into empowering facts.

ATTRACT Your Ideal Spouse
Attain clarity about your unique wants and needs in a relationship by using these tools to visualize and articulate your vision.

My Happiness Journal
Imagine it's already happened! Clarify your vision to attract your ideal spouse into your life.

Dream Board
Use this display as a tool to visual your dreams and realize them (and have fun in the process).

Marriage Vision
Articulate your:
• Emotional needs
• Values
• Goals
• Personality

ACT in the Present
Be in action consistent with your vision by dating for marriage using a principled approach.

Commitment to Success & Dating Plan of Action
Make a commitment! Go for success by dating with structure. Date with a plan and fill your calendar with SMART goals to keep you motivated, positive, and organized.

Dating Toolkit
Be empowered and confident when dating for marriage with the philosophy, steps, how-to's, and the most commonly asked questions about dating for marriage.

Innovative Dating Tips & Slogans
Practical tips, wisdom, and coaching to support you on your dating journey of "being" the one to find the one for you!

5

Why Marry?

That is what marriage really means:
helping one another to reach the full status of being
persons, responsible and autonomous beings
who do not run away from life.

—Paul Tournier

Times have changed. You don't need to marry to increase or secure your social status, to ensure your physical safety, or to procreate. Many women (and sometimes even men) choose to have children on their own. With

115

women's improved economic standing and the elimination of much of the stigma attached to remaining single, marriage rates have declined in recent decades.

In spite of the media's negative messages, stereotypical depictions of gender roles, and reduced social pressure, people want to be married. *Yes, we still want it.* Why? We crave a human connection and a loving bond with another. We crave love and companionship; as "unnecessary" as it is, we were built for it, and we need it. We need the feedback, companionship, and emotional connection. In the words of Harold S. Kushner, "Love is the most accessible way we have of being supremely important in another person's life. It meets our need to matter. . . . We cannot live without the knowledge that someone cares about us, and marriage provides the most accessible way of having that need met. Various alternatives to marriage (including living together without ceremony and with both partners having the freedom to leave whenever they feel their needs not being met) have never managed to be as nourishing to the soul as the thousands-of-years-old institution of marriage. The alternatives carry a message of "you can be replaced" instead of "you matter to me more than anyone else in the world."[10]

In his bestselling book, *Getting the Love You Want*, Harville Hendrix says, "Many people are cynical about relationships; but it's only in a relationship where we get to heal our childhood wounds and feel true connectedness. We are all looking for the

---

10 Kushner, Harold S. *Living a Life that Matters*. Knopf, 2001. p.115.

feeling of joyful bliss, like when we were fully taken care of in the womb. We long for the spiritual feeling that all is right in the world, like when we see a sunset or new baby."

A Spiritual Soul Connection

Most world religions have promoted marriage from their inception. Jewish mystics explain that two primary considerations drive the soul's desire to marry: a desire to be complete and its need to transcend itself. Christians believe that marriage is a gift from God. Hindus also view marriage as a sacred duty for both religious and social reasons. Various groups view marriage as a sacred institution, a sacrament, or a covenant. The love between a man and a woman is indicative of the eternal love that God has for all humankind.

According to Kabbalah (ancient Jewish mysticism), the compulsion to rush into a lifelong commitment is an expression of the human soul's deepest ambitions. The hidden signals emanating from the soul have caused marriage to be a vital part of human society since the dawn of time. The soul's desire to connect makes the aspiration for marriage one of our most basic instincts.

In the first marriage ever, Adam and Eve were initially created as a single body. The single being was split in two—a man and a woman—and then reunited in matrimony. The attraction to the opposite sex actually stems from the soul's innate desire to reunite with its soul mate. The Talmud says that each soul's *bashert* (predestined soul mate) is determined before its birth. The two may be born continents apart with seemingly nothing in common, but Divine destiny ensures that everyone's path intersects with their *bashert*'s.[11]

When Martin Buber, the great Jewish philosopher and theologian, was asked, "Where is God?" he gave a remarkable answer: that God lives in relationships. God is not found *in* people, but God is found *between* people. When you and I are truly attuned to each other, God comes down and fills the space between us so that we are connected, not separated.[12] In her course, "Adventures in Intimacy," Hedy Schleifer teaches that concept experientially. She leads couples to experience the true meaning of empathy and generosity using a technique called "crossing the bridge" over to your partner's world, creating a relational space as a way of being truly generous and present for them. In the exercise that borrows from Martin Buber's[13] idea that the space between a couple is sacred, couples can communicate their needs, wishes, and desires safely and openly because when crossing the bridge, we leave our own concerns behind so we can hear fully what the other is communicating. Often the communication is a request to be heard or for an unconditional emotional gift from our partner that may be an unfulfilled need from childhood.

And when we maintain the awareness that we each carry a

---

11 http://www.chabad.org/library/article_cdo/aid/448425/jewish/Why-Marry.htm.

12 Kushner, Harold S. *Living a Life that Matters*. Knopf, 2001. p. 124.

13 Martin Buber was an Austrian-born Jewish philosopher best known for his philosophy of dialogue, a form of religious existentialism centered on the distinction between the I-Thou relationship and the I-It relationship.

small child within us, and that our future partner also carries special needs from his or her childhood, we have the capacity to be generous, mature, and empathetic. This is the ultimate experience of love and connection.

Practical Reasons to Marry

On a practical level, marriage promotes personal growth in two ways: we learn to accommodate our spouse's needs and we benefit by the encouragement of our spouse's nurturance. Married individuals often find that because of a spouse's support and encouragement, they are able to pursue goals and interests they might not have otherwise followed.[14]

The quality of our lives and physical health is also tied to our closest relationships. In "How to Live to be 100+," *National Geographic* columnist Dan Buettner's study found that genetics account for only 10 percent of how long the average person lives, and that what accounted for 90 percent was the lifestyle of people who had deep connections with friends, family, and community.[15] Richard Koch, author of the bestselling book *The 80/20 Principle*[16] suggests "developing a close relationship with a happy partner" as a vehicle to living a happy life. He

---

14 Rosie Einhorn, LCSW, and Sherry Zimmerman, J. D., M.Sc. http://www.aish.com/d/a/103034994.html.

15 In his September 10, 2009, TED.com talk, "How to Live to be 100+," *National Geographic* columnist Dan Buettner references the "Danish Twin" study.

16 The principle was suggested by management thinker Joseph M. Juran. It was named after an idea from the Italian economist Vilfredo Pareto who observed that 80 percent of income in Italy was received by 20 percent of the Italian population. The assumption is that most of the results in any situation are determined by a small number of causes.

states, "The selection of a partner is one of the few decisions in life (one of the 20 percent) that will help determine whether we are happy or not." He also suggests a shortcut to lasting happiness is to *evolve the lifestyle you and your partner want.* So again, identifying a partner with common vision, values, and goals is a clear path to life of happiness.

Dating for Marriage

A successful marriage is an edifice that
must be rebuilt every day.

—André Maurois

Dating for the purpose of marriage has been done for centuries, and the best of its principles are timely and can be applied successfully in modern times. As we've discussed, dating no longer has to involve superficial meetings based on common interests, flirting, and chemical attraction. With a process designed for people to build lasting marriages, dating can be elevated to a meaningful experience.

In conventional dating scenarios, a discussion of marriage is vague at best, typically mentioned only as a concept. Core issues about values, hopes, dreams, aspirations, family issues, children, finances, where to live, where to travel, consideration of working as partners, and other preferences are just not usually discussed. Thirty-something singles who put careers first want a bottom-line approach to dating. They don't want to waste time with the wrong people, and they don't want to wait around trying to guess whether the person across the table shares a similar vision and goals for the future.

Never Marry "Potential"[17]

I often ask people who are divorced if they were confident they knew all of the important things when they walked down the aisle. The answer is usually no. I regularly hear, "Well, I didn't really like how we differed in our approach to handling finances" or "He didn't want children, but I figured he would change his mind." Almost all of them told me that they did have doubts. There were questions about whether their hopes and dreams meshed with that of their partner. There were concerns that they were too afraid to address. Did they like their future spouse's personality? Did they admire him or her? Did they share a common vision and goals? They hoped for the best.

Many were afraid of the answers, or if they knew something wasn't quite right, it was too late to back out since the invitations were already mailed or the hall was already filled with guests. Despite the doubts, they proceeded with trepidation and hope— hope that the person would change and hope that the vision would come together.

Because the couples either didn't agree or didn't discuss core issues early on, there was a strong possibility for failure. The

---

17 Rabbi Dov Heller, "Ten Ways to Marry the Wrong Person," http://www.aish.com/d/w/489 55756.html.

initial attraction and passion that brings most modern couples together doesn't address what's most important when the initial spell wears off.

I embarked upon a quest to understand what made great marriages. Interviewing scores of people, I found a common thread among couples who were married for a long time. This helped me understand what was going on when they met and what worked about it.

Twenty-First-Century Dating-for-Marriage Model

Much of my research came from a group of people who successfully date for marriage. The stories are nothing short of inspirational. I found that the more traditional approaches of dating for marriage in a segment of the Orthodox Jewish world, specifically the Chabad[18] community, work phenomenally well in creating dynamic, successful partnerships. Why? The couples are not dating in a superficial way, so they eliminate much of the pain and confusion that singles otherwise go through.

Singles of all religions and backgrounds can benefit from this time-tested dating system and use elements of it to produce long-lasting, authentic partnerships. The key elements to emulate for this kind of marriage-minded dating include:

---

18 According to the Chabad-Lubavitch website (www.chabad.org), Chabad-Lubavitch "is a philosophy, a movement, and an organization. It is considered to be one of the most dynamic forces in Jewish life today. The movement's system of Jewish religious philosophy, the deepest dimension of G-d's Torah, teaches understanding and recognition of the Creator, the role and purpose of creation, and the importance and unique mission of each creature. This philosophy guides a person to refine and govern his or her every act and feeling through wisdom, comprehension, and knowledge."

1. Seek out and use a successful, happily married and experienced mentor.
2. Do research in advance and meet only after establishing that you could be a good match (based on common vision, values, goals, admiration, and inspiration).
3. Keep the first meeting short to see if there's a spark.
4. Have authentic, meaningful conversations.
5. Maintain physical boundaries—this is a potential spouse.
6. Have faith that you will meet the right one.

It's important to note that the Hollywood depiction of old-country "shtetl" matching is a far cry from the dating-for-marriage scenario I'm describing here. Rather, it is an exciting pursuit by consenting adults who are dating according to certain principles.

You may think that dating for marriage is impersonal and unromantic. This couldn't be further from the truth! For singles, it's very exciting and romantic to date to meet people and discuss possibilities. Searching for your life partner and getting to know him or her is romantic, as you will learn from those who have experienced it. Here's how it works.

Mentors

People who know singles best and care about them are their supportive advocates. These may be parents, friends, and siblings, or even teachers and rabbis, all who can network to think of potential matches. By acting as matchmakers, the marriage-minded singles are set up by the people who know them best and not by strangers. These mentors are best able to scrutinize the personality traits and goals of potential matches.

Because the community is close-knit yet global, the reach for potential matches is vast. All the mentors keep the single person in mind, asking, "Who do I know that would be good for so and so?" Even more important, "She has this kind of personality and really needs somebody with these qualities. . . ."

In addition, most children in these communities are raised to know that marriage is a beautiful and sacred institution. They understand from a young age that relationships are built over time on a strong foundation. They receive positive messages about marriage all of their lives, especially from their parents and their mentors. When children regularly experience how their parents bring together the important elements of their lives, whether it is the beauty and warmth of Shabbat meals, opening their homes to guests, or abiding by the commitments involved in living a life of gratitude, they naturally have a positive view of marriage. They are very likely going to want to create the relationships their parents had for themselves. For better or worse, children learn what they live, and a good example has resonating effects.

For the singles who join the community as adults and who weren't raised with these examples, their advocates are the ones who are there supporting them in their spiritual development: friends, rabbis, and teachers. Anyone who is dating for marriage should have a mentor—someone who has a great marriage and who can provide open and honest feedback.

Research and the Decision to Meet

In the typical situation, the couples research each other before they meet. Whether or not they meet at all depends on having all the important questions answered. These questions relate to family background, education, personality, values, goals, and sensibilities. By using this approach, they already know quite a bit about each other when they first meet. This research can be emulated by all singles, regardless of how they meet. Through conversation and comparison of vision, values, and goals, important criteria will surface early, making the decision of whether to meet in person very clear.

The first date is kept lighthearted. The singles first look for attraction, chemistry, and flow of conversation. A marriage must start with at least some spark, which can eventually ignite into fire and passion; the marriage probably won't work if it's missing. Another element of the date is to see if the singles like and enjoy each other's personalities.

Meaningful Conversations

For singles looking for the one who is right for them, seeking out authentic romance is rewarding in and of itself. The dating is genuine and real, and for people who want to get married, the possibilities are endless.

Singles of all backgrounds of any religion who are serious about marriage can date in a meaningful way, and that is what *Meet to Marry* is about. Having open and honest conversations with realistic expectations (i.e., don't look for love at first sight, because it's typically not enduring) is the right approach from the start.

We all know those happily married couples who say that they love their spouse more today than when they met. When singles are matched in this community, they are prepared. They know themselves well, and they know what they are looking for in a marriage partner.

One matchmaker I interviewed explained that when a person can articulate the kind of person they'd like to meet and has a clear vision, their chances of finding a perfect match are great. It's the clear vision, combined with knowing oneself, that allows matchmakers and mentors to find suitable matches—that and intuition, of course.

Maintain Physical Boundaries

Many people experience disappointment from looking for love in all the wrong places. Intimacy before there is caring and commitment can be a big problem because it often precludes a fully honest exploration of important issues. Physical involvement tends to cloud one's mind. And a clouded mind is not inclined to make good decisions.

It is not necessary to take a "test drive" in order to find out if a couple is physically compatible. If you do your homework and make sure you are intellectually and emotionally compatible, you don't have to worry about it. Of all the studies done on divorce, incompatibility in the "physical intimacy" arena is almost never cited as a main reason why people divorce.[19]

While this might seem radical, different, or unreasonable for some, most women will agree that once they enter a physical relationship, things do become clouded. Most men also respect women who maintain their boundaries. Too many people confuse sex and love. Holding off on physical intimacy until there is a commitment makes sense. You'll have a lifetime of intimacy once you find the right mate.

Have Faith

What determined, serious singles have in common is a tremendous faith that they will meet the right person. It's uncanny. They have faith that with their strong desire, combined with action, they will meet their *bashert*, their fated soul mate.

A Case for Marrying Young

In modern dating scenarios, singles wait to get married until everything is "right." They wait until they have a certain amount of money in the bank, finish their education, travel the

---

19 Rabbi Dov Heller, "Ten Ways to Marry the Wrong Person." http://www.aish.com/d/w/48955756.html.

world, or reach a certain age due to a societal emphasis on self-actualization and fulfillment. But many later ask, "Is everything ever right?"

While the idea of marrying young is not for everyone, it's worth consideration. Many people, upon reaching a certain age, feel a sense of loss, panic, and regret about not having married and started a family earlier. I personally know the pain of having waited, and looking back at my earlier "feminist" view on things, I feel a more traditional approach makes far more sense for me. I don't feel the need to compete with men, and I embrace my own uniqueness as a woman who loves business and working, but more important, nurturing.

An alternative to this pattern of waiting is to create a future with a partner early on. The advantages are many. When younger, couples are usually at optimal fertility. Stress levels are reduced, and as such the couple has more energy to devote to their marriage as well as their careers and other interests. Finally, it's easier to create a life and a future together, long before the individual partners feel set in their ways. Younger couples don't wait for it to be right—they make it right. Rosie Einhorn, LCSW, and Sherry Zimmerman, J.D., M.Sc., who counsel singles, point out that with their spouse's support and encouragement, many members of couples find they are able to pursue goals and interests they might not have otherwise followed. In addition, the experience of growing with a partner, developing the art of compromise, team planning, and communication hones skills that prove invaluable in all areas of life, including the workplace. Further, parenthood (motherhood, specifically) can in fact facilitate this growth even more with its inherent call for loyalty, self-sacrifice, performing under stress, and so on. The "decision" to marry and begin a family at a young age is largely based on an individual's worldview. We are all products of our environment, and the attitudes of the society in which we live heavily influence our choices.[20]

In the twenty-first-century dating-for-marriage model, singles are able to continue the process of self-actualization and pursue their goals at the same time that they are building a marriage and a family, due to the powerful marital dynamics described above.

The Fear

It doesn't interest me how old you are.
I want to know if you will risk looking like a fool,
for love,
for your dream,
for the adventure of being alive

The Invitation, by Oriah Mountain Dreamer

---

20 Rosie Einhorn, L.C.S.W., and Sherry Zimmerman, J. D., M.Sc. http://www.aish.com/d/a/103034994.html.

Case Study:
Carol, Age Thirty, on Becoming Real

The following story demonstrates how a cynical young woman who had been dating for more than ten years came to see how her fear kept her single. Carol is a very analytical person. A social worker by profession, she is upbeat and smart, up front in her communication, and not someone you'd want to challenge to a debate. Carol is sweet, but you can't quite put your finger on what her "wall" is about. She quietly keeps her guard up; with a shy smile, occasionally becoming chatty and pleasant, she still constantly sizes up the situation. Carol thinks her critical personality is a result of her relationship with her very uncommunicative parents.

A decade into "the dating game," Carol is committed to meeting the right person and getting married, but it hasn't happened yet. Her longest relationship was a near-engagement that ended after three months. She dates frequently, but turns down around 30 percent of the men suggested to her because she's not sure they fit her criteria.

After a first date, Carol carefully reviews what happened: she analyzes what the person said, how he said it, and what it all means. Even if she senses someone is not right for her, she goes on a second date "just to make sure," because she admits she doesn't trust her instincts.

Having a lot of experience as a social worker with at-risk children, she has led a self-examined life. She notices everything about herself. When she discusses her issues, she has an excellent sense of their origins: her relationship with her mother and the type of childhood she had. She has analyzed it all, the good, the bad, and the ugly.

Exceedingly critical of her dates, Carol often wonders why she even bothered. She recounted the story of a recent date with a guy who described himself as open and self-actualized in his profile. Throughout their date, he kept explaining to her how open and self-actualized he was. Carol was annoyed: "If he was open, wouldn't he just come across that way instead of having to justify it to me?"

Carol describes the kind of men she dates, and it's all the same: "too young," "too know-it-all," "too shallow," "too closed up," and on and on.

In previous sessions with me, she resisted the coaching, objecting that many of my suggestions were "hard." She regularly challenged my suggestions with the "buts": but this, but that, but the other. I explained to her that if she wasn't coachable, a breakthrough was unlikely. Eventually, she consented since her goal was to have a breakthrough. With a smile, she decided to try, conceding that her way hadn't worked.

I asked her what she felt were her top emotional needs. She said she wanted "to be understood and loved for who I am, to meet someone who will understand me, someone really warm and compassionate."

In response, I asked her the following series of questions:

- When you are on a date, are you understanding?
- Are you warm?
- Are you open, kind, and understanding to the person you are meeting?
- Or do you attract guys who are tough, superficial, or analytical?
- Who do you not want to see more than once?
- Who do you have to protect yourself from?
- With whom do you feel misunderstood?
- Who reminds you of your withdrawn parents?
- If anything, are the guys you attract *the opposite of what you want*?
- In fact, could these guys be *just like you*?

Carol started to understand where I was going. Her face softened.

After she thought about her responses to these questions, we proceeded to examine "the story" she had made up about herself. Looking at her childhood as the origin of her issues, she realized her reaction to her withdrawn and uncommunicative parents was a desperate desire to be understood. She felt alone. She felt that nobody listened to her. She felt that she wasn't loved so she was unlovable.

Carol agreed that "I am unlovable" was the essence of the story she made up about herself. Her mother has always been very critical of her, and she lacked a sense of intimacy with her family. By uncovering the root of her problems, Carol could now understand that this story she had created about herself at a young age was simply not the truth. As a grown woman, I explained, she has the ability to invent a new, more powerful way to relate to herself.

I asked her what would happen if she could *be* that person she really was inside. I asked her what would happen if she could disconnect from her negative childhood story that keeps her on the defensive, believing that nobody can understand her and love her. Deep down, was her essence pessimistic and critical? Her answer, of course, was no. So I asked Carol to consider switching modes, to envision a big, joyful future for herself.

In *Keeping the Love You Find,* Harville Hendrix states that we are all looking for a sense of connectedness. The entire universe is connected, and we see it so clearly in nature. But when we leave the womb and grow up, we have experiences that we add our own meaning to, and in time, we lose the feeling of connectedness and begin putting up walls and defenses. It is these walls and defenses that keep us far removed from the happiness we so desperately want.

Carol and I talked about spirituality and joy. I asked her to remember a time when she felt that everything was wonderful in the world, when she felt happy and safe, a time when she didn't have to protect herself; a time when all was good.

We came to the conclusion that if she were a loving, open, and warm person, she would then attract men who were also loving, open, and warm. I asked her to contemplate a few words that might resonate for her. I suggested *vulnerable.* She added *connected, generous,* and *joyful.*

Vulnerable

I suggested that she attempt to consciously connect to these emotions. She asked me if being vulnerable means being unsafe. I explained that being vulnerable means being open, without walls, without the armor of protection she'd been carrying for so long. Being vulnerable would allow her to be safe in her skin, a feminine quality, the opposite of being tough (as she has been).

Connected

Her next word, *connected*, means having a connection to herself and her world without judging and analyzing everything. Being connected means not defining things as being "good" or "bad." When people are connected to themselves and the world, there is space for faith to trust that everything is for the good, that there's always something to be grateful for, even a first date sitting across the café table. When the walls come down, people see their dates as unique, richly blessed human beings, whether or not they are the right match.

Generous

Generosity is being free to share yourself and who you are with others. People are capable of giving others the space to reciprocate too. If Carol could be generous, she would be able to attract men who were also generous. Her face again softened, and she agreed that she could be.

As a person who works with troubled children, Carol could

very much understand that she was already contributing to others. She was already a generous person. Referring back to her work, I asked her if she told the children she counsels that their lives would always be awful and that they should think small and be critical of themselves and others. She responded that of course she didn't! Then why did *she* say those things to herself?

Carol needed to develop a big vision for her life, one that would be stronger than her inner voice. In doing so, she would have the power to sustain a new practice of noticing when she was using her negative, analytical voice.

To stay in that mind-set, I instructed her to listen to podcasts and read books by some of the world's most acclaimed positive-thought leaders, including Steven Covey, Mark Victor Hansen, Anthony Robbins, Bob Proctor, Zig Ziglar, and others every day, without exception. I also suggested using 12-step slogans like "Lighten up!" and "Easy does it."

Finally, I suggested that she begin to develop a sense of compassion for herself and others. The ability to see herself as a little child was crucial. She needed to treat herself as she would treat her at-risk clients: with love and respect. It was Carol's opportunity to nurture that little girl inside of her, the one who found a way to cope by being tough, putting up walls, and beating up herself and others. As an adult, she doesn't need those walls. She can take care of herself.

With this breakthrough, her new vision, and all of the tools at her disposal, Carol could get off her own back and practice being in the zone of what she called "the magic of positivity," a place she now knew was nothing but a choice. Little by little, day by day, all of us can learn to nurture ourselves and to take on practices that demonstrate unconditional self-love. Such simple yet profound practices are the foundation to vibrate positivity and achieve clarity in attracting "the one" we desire into our lives.

I asked Carol, "How can you expect to receive from someone else that which you won't give to yourself?" Each time she responded, "But it will be hard." I replied to her, "Yes, I know that it won't be easy, but it will be worth it." Self-love, like everything else, is a practice that we need to bring to our awareness every hour of every day.

Reminders, slogans, notes, and healthy regular practices such as prayer or contemplation, meditation, a hot bath, a calming walk, journaling, listening to motivational speakers, and taking time to be with friends and loved ones, can all make a difference. By taking on practices that help break down the walls of fear, defensiveness, criticism, and judgment, there will be greater space in one's heart and more room in one's soul for love and joy to exist.

You Attract What You Are Ready for and Feel You Deserve

Don't marry the person you think
you can live with; marry only the individual
you think you can't live without.

—James C. Dobson

I ran into Amanda, a successful, creative thirty-year-old, at a jazz festival. Not having seen her in quite a while, I asked her what was new in her life. After years of being attracted to "bad guys" for purely physical reasons, she had finally met someone about whom she was very serious. He seemed to have all of the qualities she was looking for. They shared a similar spiritual outlook, values, and goals. She was ready for a change.

This guy was the change she felt she needed. He was different: kind and good; she felt extremely safe with him. Trustworthy and a good soul, he wanted to marry her. Still, Amanda seemed to be struggling. I asked her why.

While he was great "on paper," and she was very excited about him and what he offered her, she was concerned that she didn't feel physically attracted to him. In her mind, she thought the attraction could grow over time. I recognized that she had some issues to confront.

We made an appointment and I started to coach her. We discussed attraction principles, and why we attract who we attract. The key principle in Amanda's case was that *we attract that which we feel we deserve.* Her previous relationships were unsatisfying, and after her most recent one, an adrenaline-filled attraction, she was ready for someone safe. Because she was needy and wanted to be with someone who could take care of her, Amanda attracted only part of what she needed in a relationship—a good person with similar values, vision, and goals for the future, *but no attraction.*

Physical attraction, or a lack thereof, it turned out, was a deal-breaker. If she couldn't imagine being intimate with him, it could never work, nor was it likely to grow over time. The break-through? Her neediness attracted someone like a brother or a father.

In his book *Doesn't Anyone Blush Anymore?*, Manis Friedman explains why family relationships are calm (at least compared to love relationships, generally speaking). They come easy because brothers, sisters, parents, and children are traditionally very familiar and typically feel comfortable with one another. In a marriage, a husband and wife were once strangers. Male is differ-ent from female, as well; so, in essence, they must remain strang-ers. Because of this fundamental difference, the love between them can never be casual, consistent, or calm. This "acquired" love is naturally more intense than the love between brother and sister. When love has to overcome a difference, a distance, or an obstacle, it needs energy to leap across and bridge the gap. According to Friedman, "This is the energy of fiery love."

After several coaching sessions, Amanda had a break-through. She created her My Happiness & Finding My Life Partner Journal, her Marriage Vision, and her Dating Plan of Action. She raised her self-esteem through the process and took new actions that were consistent with her vision. Suddenly, everything changed! She was clear about the kind of husband and partner she wanted. She let go of her neediness and began to value herself and her needs. She had a total shift in her expe-rience of life and dating, *and* she noticed things changing based on her new awareness. She began meeting available, appropri-

ate men, and then six months later, she finally met "the one."
Amanda is now engaged with plans to be married soon.

Relationship and "Life Design" Tools

The first step in designing your future is to create your My Happiness & Finding My Life Partner Journal. This will help you to create clarity about your vision for your future, and for the kind of person you want to attract into your life.

You can design your life from scratch by being very clear about what you want and desire. After completing this exercise honestly and with intentionality, expect to have breakthroughs and big "aha" moments. Many singles have reported that after the experience of creating the journal, their lives began to shift and their desires started manifesting in reality.

The first step is to get a journal; any nice notebook will do. Label it clearly as "My Happiness & Finding My Life Partner Journal." (Visit www.MeetToMarry.com to create your personalized journal). Creating a journal will allow you to focus your energy on the future you want, and it will provide you with the vision of the kind of person you want to be and who you'll attract into your life.

Introductory note: People attract what they are ready for at any given time. If we don't attract something or someone we desire, it's because this idea or person is not yet in our awareness, whether it's money, people, or circumstances. You are a unique person with specific emotional needs and goals, and by putting your vision in writing, you will clarify your dream for yourself. The universe and your psyche will become clear.

Have a Breakthrough! Create Your
My Happiness & Finding My Life Partner Journal

Get your pen ready! Remember to come from a new, blank space not dictated by the past or any story you used to tell yourself. Allow your new empowering story to convey what's in your heart, mind, and soul. Know that you deserve happiness and to find meaningful, lasting love in your life. This has always been the *true* story.

Write down exactly what you are looking for and what your life will look like when you are married. Remember, it's your life to design, once you understand and embrace universal attraction principles, the universe will bring to you what you want—at the time that is right for you. You need to be very clear. To complete this exercise, carve out a little quiet time and find a space where you will not be interrupted. Give yourself permission to be creative and brutally honest. No holds barred. Go for the gold—it's your life!

1. *Think of a date you would like to be married by.* Write it down. By choosing a date, your energy and actions will align.

      Today's date: _____

      I will be married by: _____

2. *Stand in the future looking back as though it's already happened, and imagine your life.* You've already chosen your wedding date. Imagine that wedding. How will it feel? Who is there? Hear the music, see the people, and notice the scenery. Allow yourself to be creative in the process, and let your body feel all of the sensations and as much of the joy and love as possible. Stay in this place of pure creativity as you continue the exercise.

_____

_____

_____

_____

_____

_____

_____

_____

_____

"Begin with the End in Mind" is Habit 2 of the bestselling *7 Habits of Highly Effective People*, in which Steven Covey describes a process based on imagination—the ability to envision in your mind what you cannot at present see with your eyes. It is based on the principle that all things are created twice. There is a mental creation (first) and a physical creation (second). The physical creation follows the mental, just as a building follows a blueprint. If you don't make a conscious effort to visualize who you are and what you want in life, then you empower other people and circumstances to shape you and your life by default. It's about connecting again with your own uniqueness and then defining the personal, moral, and ethical guidelines within which you can most happily express and fulfill yourself. "Begin with the End in Mind" means to begin each day, task, or project with a clear vision of your desired direction and destination, and then continue by flexing your proactive muscles to make things happen.[21]

3. *How would you like to feel in a relationship?* What is the person like? What is your life together like? How do you relate to each other and what things do you do together? Imagine the body sensation of being with your ideal partner. Imagine laughing or playing or dancing. What does it feel like to have your needs met? How does it feel to be fulfilled?

_____

_____

_____

_____

_____

_____

_____

4. *What will your life together be like?* How do you imagine your family life? How do you imagine your spiritual life? Will you be surrounded by children, will you have combined families, extended family? Will you have pets? How does it feel to be a part of this family?)

_____

_____

_____

_____

_____

21 *The 7 Habits of Highly Effective People* by Steven Covey has sold more than 15 million copies worldwide since its first publication in 1989.

5. *How do you express appreciation for each other? What do you* appreciate about each other? How do you express your needs and desires? How does it feel to be able to express yourself fully and to ask for what you need?

_____

_____

_____

6. *How do you play together and enjoy each other's company?* What do you do for fun and recreation? Do you travel together? What type of places do you visit? What's the scenery like?

_____

_____

_____

7. *Continue to imagine and write down anything else that is* *important to you and continue to use this journal as new* *ideas, dreams, and wishes emerge.*

_____

_____

_____

Mitch (who you met in Chapter 3) was asked to complete the journal exercise, and when I asked him what date he chose to be married by, he looked at me blankly. "You want me to write down a date?" he asked.

"Absolutely," I told him.

He didn't understand that he could create his future. To help him understand, I explained it in a different way. "Mitch, you are a computer programmer, right? When you write software, do you just start coding and hope that the code does what you want it to do? Would you achieve the desired outcome that way? Of course not!"

Mitch told me that he works with specifications and requirements. (Obviously!) He knew what he wanted each specific piece of software to do, so he basically worked backward from the end point, always keeping that in mind. Mitch designed his programs on paper with the desired outcomes and features, used a methodology, and then sat down and began the process. This exercise utilizes the same idea.

By choosing a date, you can better see the vision, feel the vision, and then be inspired to live your life in a manner consistent with meeting that goal. This is a future not dictated by the past nor generated by dysfunctional thinking. The dream and the vision are a *million* times bigger than your negativity!

Your brain already gets it. You start to live your life, not as a skeptical, disillusioned person, but as a person who has achieved the goal already . . . and now you can perform the actions associated with the dream. People will see you differently. You will become positive by surrounding yourself with positive people and activities, and your life will start to change—*all because you chose a date.* Be excited! *Dream big!*

Date to Marry Tip: Trust your instincts; your "gut" is never wrong.

If someone looks great on paper, but you don't feel it, don't second-guess yourself. It's not worthwhile. We all know what it feels like when it seems like someone should be perfect, but you feel that "something's not quite right." The good news is you're definitely not missing out. He/she is just not right for you. Your instincts and your intuition are telling you so. Move on.

6

Visualize Your Dreams to Attract Your Ideal Spouse

To love and be loved is to feel the
sun from both sides.

—David Viscott

*I have come to the frightening conclusion
that I am the decisive element. It is my personal
approach that creates the climate. It is my daily mood that
makes the weather. I possess tremendous power to make
life miserable or joyous. I can be a tool of torture*

or an instrument of inspiration. I can humiliate or humor,
hurt or heal. In all situations, it is my response
that decides whether a crisis is escalated or de-escalated,
and a person is humanized or dehumanized.
If we treat people as they are, we make them worse.
If we treat people as they ought to be, we help them
become what they are capable of becoming.

—Johann Wolfgang von Goethe

In the movie *Solitary Man*, Michael Douglas plays a formerly successful owner of car dealerships who falls into shame and gives up his life and family to spend his time picking up women and having meaningless affairs. Always disappointing his grown daughter, he's constantly late to visit his grandson, hits up his daughter for loans, and finally sinks so low as to seduce his own girlfriend's college-age daughter. In one powerful scene, Douglas meets up with an old friend from his alma mater, played by Danny DeVito, a family man who leads a much simpler life, running a deli in the same college town in which they met. When Douglas hits hard times, DeVito gives him a job. One day, standing behind the counter, they have a conversation about life. Douglas, admiring a table filled with pretty young students, says to DeVito, "Isn't it tempting to be around all of these young, pretty girls all the time?"

Devito responds by saying, "Look, I watch these girls over the four years they are in college, and they are just that—pretty girls passing through. On the other hand, my wife, she's my best friend . . . and you know what? We continue to have great conversations after all of these years."

Maturity: A Key Element of Marriage Readiness

What makes a person ready? The key elements to marriage readiness are maturity, generosity, and self-awareness: knowing your own "stuff." As Manis Friedman points out in his book *Doesn't Anyone Blush Anymore?*, "to be devoted to a relationship means to be devoted to the other person's needs even more so than your own. It means taking on the other person's needs as though they were yours. In doing so, two people merge into one. And when couples have this feeling of oneness, they have a foundation to build a life."[22]

Marriage takes the 1+1=1 approach. As the saying goes, a couple arrives at the doctor's office and when asked what the problem is, the husband says, "Doctor, our foot hurts." Through life's experience and bonding, two become one.

Being the right partner means being mature enough to know that a good marriage requires commitment, discipline, and the courage to grow and change. Marriage-ready maturity is not age-dependent at all. I've met people in their twenties who are emotionally more mature and ready for marriage than some people in their forties or even fifties.

---

22 The central theme of this work is modesty. The author explains how modesty, often dismissed as irrelevant, can become a powerful tool for forming lasting relationships. His book attempts to redirect our thinking about sexuality and refocus our ideas about intimacy.

Eli Levy, Ph.D., suggests that having integrity and trust in yourself and your partner, and then stepping into marriage is itself what makes you marriage-ready. You must have faith in yourself and in your partner to know that your feelings are genuine, and that you are truly present. It comes down to the authenticity and integrity of the self—and the willingness to leap.

In addition, we can heal our childhood wounds in a marriage. When we are with our spouses, we can stretch, grow, and truly become complete human beings. There's no "tension" or stretching when we are alone. When alone, we basically do what we want to do, and there is no mirror—no reflection from another person. Marriage is the ultimate personal growth experience. It is challenging at times? Of course. All worthwhile endeavors are and that's why commitment is necessary. As long as there's an escape route, a person will take it when the going gets rough. When there's no escape route, a person will tap every bit of his/her potential to fight for victory.[23] And the rewards of loving another and being loved are worth it.

Generosity

As human beings we need not only to feel loved and "to be somebody's somebody"[24] but we need to give and be generous; to make a difference in someone's life. As Dr. Dean Ornish

---

23 http://www.aish.com/f/m/84558807.html by Sara Yoheved Rigler "Why Marriage Matters." A Jewish response to Elizabeth Gilbert's bestseller.
24 Kushner, Harold S. *Living a Life that Matters.* Knopf, 2001. pg 112.

says, "Our survival depends on the healing power of love, intimacy, and relationships" but true love also involves nourishing someone else's soul, not only finding someone to nourish yours. Ornish writes, "I used to feel I was loved because I was special, now I feel special because I am loved and because I *can* love." The more love we want, the more generous we should be and eliminate the "what have you done for me lately" attitude that is so prevalent in our society today. Even more, we must take on a practice of seeing ourselves and our loved ones as "new" every day with a feeling of gratitude. Do you know why parents love their children more than children love their parents? It's because parents have been giving and generous to their children since the children were born. John F. Kennedy once said, "Ask not what your country can do for you; ask what you can do for your country." The same is true in creating powerful relationships.

Choose Love

Love is the attachment that results from deeply appreciating another's goodness. We can choose love and choose to be loving at any time. Being loving is active. The access to it is by focusing on the goodness of a person.

In her article "What Is Love?," Gila Manolson asked a group of high school students what their idea of love was. At first, they had no response, so she offered up, "Love is that feeling you get when you meet the right person."Every hand went up, and she thought, "Oh my!"

This is how many people approach a relationship. Consciously or unconsciously, we believe love is a sensation (based on physical and emotional attraction) that is magically, spontaneously generated when "Mr. or Ms. Right" appears.

Just as easily, love can spontaneously degenerate when the magic "just isn't there" anymore.[25] You fall in love, and you can fall out of it. But a mature, committed person can choose love at any moment. There's an expression that says "You can be right, or you can have love." I say, choose love.

How Do We Fall in Love?

When we fall in love, we feel as though we are high—we're on a "love drug." We say, "I feel like I've known you my whole life." The reason we feel that is because we have. Here's how it works. In a world of 7 billion people, we are looking for a love match, and our eyes scan for someone familiar. We scan people's faces and vote "no, no, no, no, no," and then suddenly someone appears and we say "Yes!" We say yes, according to psychologist Harville Hendrix, because we are looking for our "Imago" match. In Latin, *Imago* means "image." When we scan the crowd, we are unconsciously looking for someone to complete us, and who better than someone who is like our parents?

Our parents, who nurtured us and took care of us, also disappointed us. They disappointed us because they are human, and no human relationship is perfect. Approximately eighteen

---

25 Manolson, Gila. "What Is Love?" http://www.aish.com/d/w/48952241.html.

months after the love drug wears off, we find imperfections in our beloved, and the cute things about him or her that we found so endearing suddenly become annoying. We become frustrated, and as Hendrix explains, we go on autopilot—old-brain survival mode. Our past is knocking at our door. The expectation that all the inadequacies and all the incomplete bits of our lives would be fulfilled by our loved one has suddenly been shattered.

When we understand that certain fears come from within us and have nothing to do with our partner, our relationships can thrive. We are in a better position to make educated choices about who to marry. While who we marry is very important, being marriage-ready ourselves is even more important.

If you are not self-aware and do not know yourself well (i.e. your stories), you risk projecting fear and disappointment onto your beloved. When this situation arises, people who know themselves are in a far better position to take responsibility for their feelings and reactions than someone who is running unconsciously from their hidden past.

By knowing yourself, the importance of being generous and mature, your emotional needs, and your values, you will be ready to go out and choose a matching marriage partner. With greater insight and self-awareness, marriage-ready singles have a natural "antenna" for exactly what they are looking for in a life partner. Unlike the typical single person out "playing the field," they are truly ready to share their life with someone in a committed and loving relationship. This is maturity.

Here's the distinction: it's in an unconscious marriage that you believe the best way to a good marriage is to pick the right partner. In a conscious marriage, you realize you have to *be* the right partner. The journey to a conscious marriage begins with *you* as a conscious single.

Five Commandments of a Conscious Relationship

1. Thou shalt sanctify the space between you, for you and your children dwell therein.
2. Thou shalt remember the child within, for you all carry a child who is asking for love and attention.
3. Thou shalt stretch into honoring the "other" to gift them with the healing that they need, and to help you reclaim your humanity.
4. Thou shalt release your joy freely, whether you feel like it or not.
5. Thou shalt dream the biggest dream possible together with your partner.[26]

---

26 The Commandments are taken from Hedy Schleifer and are based on Harville Hendrix's Imago principles.

Your Thoughts Have Energy

As we've discussed earlier, your thoughts have energy and with new awareness and self-acceptance you can create the future you envision. It's a great time to attain clarity about the kind of person you'd like (and need) to "attract" into your life. We attract what we feel we deserve (both consciously and subconsciously) as you've read and when you are in the mode of dating, it's crucial to be aware of your "energy" and vibrations. Thoughts have energy, and we create our own realities with the thought energies we send out and attract back to us. While we attract things we want, we can also attract things we don't want, depending on the thoughts we entertain.

When you think positively and are aware of these vibrations, you will attract the same. With practice you'll begin to notice this type of "energy." You can always tell when you have good vibes with someone. It feels great. When you meet someone whose vibes are a lower vibration than yours, you can feel dragged down. When we believe anything is possible, the sky's the limit. With positive thoughts, we can change our reality. When we focus on our deficiencies, we create a negative reality, attracting negativity, for ourselves. *You* are in charge of your energy. And when you are clear about who you are and what you stand for, you will be in the driver's seat of your life and your future—an inspiring vision indeed!

Have a Breakthrough: Create Your Meet to Marry Dream Board

I love displays and possibility! I have personally seen so many miracles of people achieving their goals using this process; it's amazing and very inspiring.

Take your mental images from your My Happiness & Finding My Life Partner Journal (from Chapter 5) and have some fun creating your dream board. Print the dream board or get a big piece of oak tag and fill it with images of the future you envision. Use visuals from magazines, photographs, pictures of places you'd like to visit, and pictures of your future life. Your future begins with your thoughts and your creative expression before it manifests in the world. Put your dream board in a place where you can see it often, and make sure to specifically look at it twice a day, especially before you go to sleep.

Date to Marry Tip: Do not spend time
with negative people.

Negative people can drag you down. Don't allow negativity to exist in your "personal space." Surround yourself with positive people in all areas. You know who they are.

What does it take to have what you want? We all probably know people who dream big and live big, who have lives that seem miraculous to us. Ask yourself if they are different than you and everyone else, or do you believe they were born with special gifts most other people don't possess? Reflect honestly on how you respond to that question.

We also know people who lead "normal" lives, stay safe, and live in their comfort zone. Their faces often have smiles on them, but it's rare that you see them "squeezing the juice" out of what life has to offer, enjoying regular waves of fulfillment and success.

The success I'm speaking of is not related to money, although it can be. It's about people living a full, fun, meaningful life—on their own terms. Balanced, free, healthy, and generally happy, they're living their "mission," be it related to career, family, or their community. These are people who are fully self-expressed.

You may ask, "What does a conversation about success have to do with dating and attracting my soul mate into my life? It actually has everything to do with it. Fulfilled, happy people naturally attract good into their lives. When you're around them, your energy is boosted, and you're inspired to be at your best. Their vitality and energy jump out at you immediately, and they are the kind of people you want to surround yourself with.

Fear, negativity, defensiveness, and so-called protective mechanisms drain energy, limit the exchange of true intimacy, and squash the joy in life. Spending time around people who are overly analytical and judgmental, too, fit into this category, as they seem to repel joy.

According to Michael Losier, author of *The Law of Attraction*:

When you shift your attention to the kinds of people you DO want in your life, that shift, coupled with your clear desire to STOP attracting negative people into your life, will set the energy in motion for new results to show up. When you shift from what you don't want to what you do want, your vibration changes. And know this, you can only hold one vibration at a time! Universal Attraction Principles are always matching your vibration in any given moment.

7

Create Your
Marriage Vision

This section describes the tools you'll use to create your Marriage Vision and the elements that make up who you are (and what you need) in a relationship. In the old paradigm, you may have been unclear about your needs and what was important, so you may have attracted random people whose goals were unknown.

If you ask the average single what he or she is looking for in a spouse, it's typically a rather general statement like, "I want someone kind and generous." Or they might say, "I'm not asking for so much, just a good person." Or at the other end of the spectrum, some might say they want to meet someone smart, with an advanced degree, who likes tennis, golf, travel, and kids. Or there are those who say she must be gorgeous or he must be handsome. However, this sort of description again leaves out what is most important: the need for an emotional bond and your core values, personality, quality of character, and long-term goals.

Your needs are much more unique and specific than that, so in this section, you'll articulate it for yourself. Your Marriage Vision is composed of what you articulate in:

- ✓ My Top Five Emotional Needs Worksheet
- ✓ My Values Worksheet
- ✓ My Personality Worksheet
- ✓ Life Goals Exercise
- ✓ My Marriage Vision Summary

Your Top Five Emotional Needs

Emotional needs, as defined by Dr. Willard Harley, author of *Marriage Builders*, are needs that, "when satisfied, leave you with a feeling of happiness and contentment, and when unsatisfied, leave you with a feeling of unhappiness and frustration." By exploring and honoring your own emotional needs, you'll begin to understand the kind of the person you want to attract as a life partner.

What things are important for you to feel content? These are the needs that prospective partners need to assess to make sure they have the qualities to fulfill these needs. How do you figure out what your emotional needs are? Look back to your childhood and think of the needs your parents met, as well as the needs you wished they could have met.

If your top emotional needs are compassion, nurturing, and adventure, it would be important to identify someone who can be all three and share your needs with them. If you don't share what your needs are, you can't expect your future spouse to be a mind reader. When our needs are not being met, we cry out or act out in various ways that can be misunderstood or misinterpreted. The trick is to know what to look for in another, and to know ourselves and when our past is knocking on our door. When we're dating and high on the "love drug," everyone is on their best behavior. So with awareness of what to look for, you can have discussions and share experiences to assess if someone has the characteristics and sensibilities you both need.

Another example of how this plays out is illustrated by a woman whose top emotional needs are affection, partnership, and compassion, and her husband's emotional needs are success, appreciation, and respect. If they are not connected or aware of each other's needs, he won't connect to his wife's deep need for love and compassion and she may have difficulty connecting to his need for her appreciation, admiration, and respect. He may love his wife deeply, but the way he shows it could be different than what she needs and vice versa. With empathy, self-awareness, and generosity, the couple can learn to meet each other's needs, which is an opportunity for growth in the marriage.

Relationships work and thrive when each individual is open to growing and becoming self-aware (as discussed in the previous chapters), and even more so if each is open to learning how to love each other in the way that *they* each need to be loved.

I discovered that my top emotional needs are first and foremost to feel cherished followed by my need for compassion, partnership, and affection. My need to feel cherished stems from feeling lonely as a child—without healthy, loving, positive nurturing—and feeling like nobody "got me." This need to feel cherished never changes.

By getting to know myself and honoring this need, I was able to attract my husband, Michael, who is attuned to my emotional needs. If I have a special request I'm able to express my feelings; I don't expect him to be a mind reader. And at the end of day, we are all responsible for creating our own happiness, but it's wonderful to have your needs met by your spouse.

My husband's top five emotional needs are partnership, connection, financial stability, organization, and affection. Here's an example of how meeting each other's needs and being conscious works in our relationship. Michael was always very organized. When we met, his desk was clean and organized and his space was clutter-free. I, on the other hand maintained a storage space filled with that extra lamp and file cabinet I'd never need. In my life with Michael, I too became clutter-free, allowing us the freedom to travel and move easily without useless, unnecessary stuff. Organization does not come naturally to me—at all. Having a husband who cannot exist in disorder creates the opportunity for me to be organized as a gift to him. By always keeping our space orderly and clutter-free, I become a better, more organized person and my husband gets to feel safe and comfortable in our space. By being conscious of each other's needs, he's aware of my need to feel cherished, and I'm aware of his need for order, I am not careless about leaving stuff around the house or amassing clutter. We're not obsessive, but always try our best to be "awake" to each other's needs. This is just one very simple example of this dynamic; the growing, stretching, honoring, and generosity that occurs in our marriage, qualities that are important to look for when searching for a spouse.[27]

Take a moment and list your top five emotional needs. Focus on your childhood and go with your gut reaction.

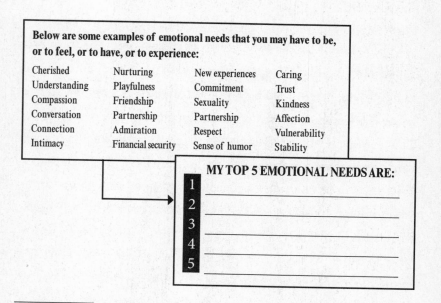

Below are some examples of emotional needs that you may have to be, or to feel, or to have, or to experience:			
Cherished	Nurturing	New experiences	Caring
Understanding	Playfulness	Commitment	Trust
Compassion	Friendship	Sexuality	Kindness
Conversation	Partnership	Partnership	Affection
Connection	Admiration	Respect	Vulnerability
Intimacy	Financial security	Sense of humor	Stability

MY TOP 5 EMOTIONAL NEEDS ARE:

1 _____
2 _____
3 _____
4 _____
5 _____

---

27 This refers to the third element of a conscious marriage based on Imago. Thou shalt stretch into honoring the "other" to gift them with the healing that they need and to help you reclaim your humanity.

Your Values

Why are values called values? *Because they are important to you!* Values are an integral part of every culture. Along with worldview and personality, they generate behavior. Values are categories that have meaning to you and color the most important choices you make in your life. Values are deeply rooted in childhood and shape who you are. People rarely compromise on their values because they are so important to a person's choices and makeup. When you are living your values, you are being true to yourself. Values can be defined as broad preferences concerning appropriate courses of action or outcomes. As such, values reflect a person's sense of right and wrong or what "ought" to be. "Equal rights for all," "Excellence deserves admiration," and "People should be treated with respect and dignity" are representative of values.[28] People who grew up in similar cultures and backgrounds begin with a common frame of reference that can provide a foundation for understanding.

Marriage is about creating harmony, interdependence, love, and partnership for the long term, so having shared values and principles creates an atmosphere of harmony and the foundation for a strong marriage. When dating for marriage and choosing a spouse, it's important to be clear about your values and the principles you believe in. Further, it's essential to find a spouse who shares the values and principles that are most important to you. When you choose a spouse who shares your values, you

---

28 Wikipedia under "values."

have agreement on the foundational themes that matter most to you both.

One friend described it well. He said that he likes spicy and his wife prefers bland; he said he's a morning person and his wife is a night person. However, in the things that matter most—like where to live and how to live, how they raise their children, and agreement on religion and managing finances—they share similar values. They are the greatest of partners, best friends, have been married for more than twenty-five years, and have three children. Since marriage is about partnership and building lifetime goals together, shared values allow you to work harmoniously together toward your vision.

Imagine you are someone who values education (for yourself, for your family, and for your community), and because you hold those values, you might choose education over material things if you had to choose (i.e., sending children to private school or saving for college). If a person who values education marries someone who doesn't share those values, there could be disagreement, conflict, and a need for much compromise. Take, for example, a person who wants children and highly values saving for the future. This person would not be well matched with someone who does not want children and prefers to live for the moment.

Articulate Your Values

Look at the following list of categories of values. Next to each item, write down what is important to you regarding those values and why. What values and principles do you stand for and hope to achieve overall? What are the guiding principles in *your* life?

Categories of values are:

Family	Contribution	Living space
Spiritual/religious	Environment	Travel
Financial/economic	Nature	Work/life balance
Political	Pets	Personal growth
Educational	Beauty &	and development
	surroundings	

Values also include ideals and character traits like:

Happiness	Warmth	Forgiveness
Generosity	Kindness	Self-control
Sensitivity	Accountability	Courage
Flexibility	Self-awareness	Politeness
Ambition	True love	Imagination
Honesty	True friendship	Independence
Humility	A meaningful life	Intellect
	Responsibility	

➤ My Values Worksheet ◄

Category	Level of importance	What do you want/how do you show those values?
Family	Very important	**Example:** I want a big family.
Spirituality/religion	Very important	**Example:** I attend religious services weekly. I was raised with a strong faith and want to meet someone to whom this is also important.
Pets	Important	**Example:** I have two dogs and value how they add to my life. I would prefer to marry someone who also values how pets add to our lives.
Politics	Not important	
Travel		
Educational		
Work/life balance		
Personal growth and development		
Contribution Charity/giving back		
Environment		
Beauty and surroundings		
Living space		

My Personality

We've discussed that in order to find a well-suited lifetime partner, it's really important to know yourself and to articulate those qualities clearly. What are your top five personality traits? Think about why you chose a certain trait and share why you chose it. For example, if you chose compassionate, you might explain your sensitivity toward others and that you volunteer with the elderly every week. If you chose creative, share how you manifest your creativity in the world. Do you paint, design, make deals, or make music?

❑ Analytical	❑ Humble	❑ Playful
❑ Adventurous	❑ Independent	❑ Resourceful
❑ Caring	❑ Intellectual	❑ Respectful
❑ Compassionate	❑ Intuitive	❑ Responsible
❑ Considerate	❑ Joyful	❑ Sarcastic
❑ Courageous	❑ Kind	❑ Sensitive
❑ Creative	❑ Laid-back	❑ Sensual
❑ Driven	❑ Leader	❑ Shy
❑ Emotional	❑ Loving	☑ Spiritual
❑ Expressive	❑ Loyal	❑ Sweet
❑ Funny	❑ Motivated	❑ Tactful
❑ Generous	❑ Nurturing	❑ Warm
❑ Grateful	❑ Optimistic	❑ Witty
❑ Helpful	❑ Outgoing	❑ Worldly
❑ Honest	❑ Passionate	

What are your top five personality traits? For each trait, explain why you chose it. How do you express this trait in the world?

Personality Trait #1: _____

I chose this trait because: _____

_____

_____

Personality Trait #2: _____

I chose this trait because: _____

_____

_____

Personality Trait #3: _____

I chose this trait because: _____

_____

_____

Personality Trait #4: _____

I chose this trait because: _____

_____

_____

Personality Trait #5: _____

I chose this trait because: _____

_____

_____

Your Inner Self:

How would you fill in the following questions so someone can get to know you? (You may even get to know yourself
a little better.)

What is most special about me: _____
_____
_____

I'll be a great spouse because: _____
_____
_____

I would like to be remembered for: _____
_____
_____

I always strive for: _____
_____
_____

My philosophy about life is: _____
_____
_____

I am most proud for having accomplished: _____
_____
_____

I am passionate about: _____
_____

What I enjoyed most about my education is: _____
_____
_____

How I help the community or the planet: _____
_____
_____

My greatest influence/mentor is (was): _____
_____
_____

What makes me most happy is: _____
_____
_____

What keeps me up at night is: _____
_____
_____

My friends would describe me as: _____
_____
_____

I would like to learn or take on: _____
_____
_____

My greatest talent is: _____
_____
_____

What Are Your Life Goals?

The final part of creating your Marriage Vision is to articulate your goals. Think back to your journal, your responses, and the items that are important to you. How do you envision your future?

My Life Goals Exercise

My Life Goals (I would like to marry someone who shares my vision and would support/share these goals):

I want/have children: _____

I envision a (small family/large family/blended family): _____

I would ideally like to live in the following location (country, city): ____
_____

The ideal setting would be (suburbs, city, beach, etc.): _____
_____

My vision of work/life balance is: _____
_____

Our spiritual life will: _____
_____

My spouse plays the following role in my life: _____
_____
_____

My spouse and I play (always together/sometimes together/
separate interests): _____
_____

I would want my spouse to share the following interest or passion
with me: _____
_____

I believe money should be: (how I save/handle money): _____
_____
_____

How my spouse and I will handle finances (jointly, separately, etc.):
_____

My travel goals are (where/how?): _____
My educational goals are: _____
_____

Personal development goals are: _____
_____

My other life goals are: _____
_____

Other elements of my marriage vision: _____
_____
_____
_____
_____
_____
_____

My Marriage Vision Summary

The Marriage Vision Summary below is a compilation of all the previous information. Use the summary to articulate who you are and what you are looking for in your ideal spouse and share with others who assist you in your search. (See page 201, Teach Others to Be Your Matchmaker.) You can also create your Marriage Vision Summary at www.MeetToMarry.com.

Facts about me:

I grew up in: _____

My religion is: _____

More about my religion observance: _____

_____

I am _____ years old.   I have _____ siblings.

My parents are (married/divorced): _____

My childhood was: _____

_____

My marital status is: _____

My marriage goal is: _____

About me (My Empowering Story from

The Reality Check in Chapter 3): _____

_____

_____

_____

My top personality traits are:

(example: funny, joyful, generous, and spontaneous)

1._____

2._____

3._____

4._____

5._____

I exhibit these traits by:

1._____

2._____

3._____

4._____

5._____

My top five emotional needs are: (the person I marry needs to be someone sensitive to these qualities):

1._____

2._____

3._____

4._____

5._____

➤ My Values ◂

Category	Importance	Why?
Family	Very important	**Example:** I want a big family
Spiritual/religion		
Education		
Charity/giving back		
The environment		
Beauty and surroundings		
Travel		
Honesty		
Humility		
Kindness		
Generosity		
Humor		

More about me:
(from Your Inner Self—Choose up to five)

What is most special about me: _____

_____

_____

I would like to be remembered for: _____

_____

_____

_____

I always strive for: _____

_____

_____

My philosophy about life is: _____

_____

_____

I am most proud for having accomplished: _____

_____

_____

I am passionate about: _____

_____

_____

What I enjoyed most about my education is: _____

_____

_____

How I help the community or the planet: _____

_____

_____

_____

My greatest influence/mentor is (was): _____

_____

What makes me most happy is: _____

_____

_____

_____

What keeps me up at night is: _____

_____

_____

_____

My friends would describe me as: _____

_____

_____

I would like to learn or take on: _____

_____

_____

My greatest talent is: _____

_____

_____

_____

_____

What to Look for in a Marriage Partner

We've come to the heart of the matter: "How will you know if someone is right for you?" What you read next may go against the traditional advice you've been receiving. The following questions will eliminate the confusion and guesswork you've been dealing with all this time.

Instead of superficial conversation and pure chemical attraction, you'll be able to answer these questions by having meaningful conversations with clarity, because you know yourself and you are free to be you. As you go through the process of meeting new people and having these meaningful conversations, the following are the points to ask yourself in order to assess if they could be an appropriate marriage partner. By testing the following conditions to see if they are true, you can identify if there is a foundation to build a lifetime partnership with someone. This tool and these criteria will give you a clear picture of what kind of person is "just right" for you:

1. Find someone whose personality you love. A personality is not something that will change. It's really important that you appreciate someone's personality as it is and the person as he/she is (both inside and out). Can you communicate deeply with this person? Do you feel an attraction and an emotional bond?

2. Find someone you admire (would want to be like). Imagine what it would be like to share your life with someone whose personal qualities you respect and admire. Does this

person exhibit the personal qualities and values that are important to you? Does he/she have the capacity to meet your emotional needs—and do you have what it would take to meet theirs to create empathy and a strong connection?

3. Find someone with common vision, values, and goals. When you marry someone who shares your vision, values, and goals, life becomes a great adventure of passion, teamwork, life-building, and communication. Does this person share your vision of the future related to family, religion, money, and where and how to live both long-term and short-term? Does your vision align?

In his article "Ten Ways to Marry the Wrong Person," Rabbi Dov Heller says, "This is the true definition of a 'soul mate.' A soul mate is a goal mate—two people who ultimately share the same understanding of life's purpose and therefore share the same priorities."

In Esther Jungreis's book, *The Committed Life*, she advises you to "find someone good, with a kind, sincere heart and go from there." Does it really matter if you are interested in golf and he/she is interested in sailing? You can always teach someone how to play tennis or sail, but you can't change someone's essence.

Topics for Meaningful Conversations

You may ask how to assess someone's values related to honesty, kindness, generosity, sensitivity, warmth, and goodness, and other values. The best way is to spend time with the person to understand what she/he is about and again have meaningful conversations. Ask questions from "Your Inner Self" section on page 172 to keep the conversations meaningful and interesting. Ask questions about family, where they grew up, what lights them up, what is important to them, what or who impacted them the most, how they enjoyed their education, if they could do anything, what would it be, what they like to be remembered for, how do they picture their future, what is their greatest strength, etc. Be creative. Meaningful questions will create meaningful conversations. Listen for inspiration, admiration, and flow—things that are important to you. Use these as guidelines to keep conversations away from the superficial conversation and surface icebreakers that keep people from getting to know core character traits that are important to you.

- *Warmth:* Does this person enjoy doing good things for other people? Do you have the experience of warmth and sensitivity in your conversations?
- *Honesty:* Does this person believe that "doing the right thing" is important?
- *Humility:* Is this person humble versus full of ego?
- *Happiness:* Does he/she enjoy life? Is he/she balanced? Do you feel comfortable being yourself and free to express yourself?

- *Generosity:* Does he/she donate his time or money to help others? Is he/she generous? Are you inspired? Is he/she a generous listener?
- *Accountability:* Does this person do what he/she says he/she's going to do? Can you count on this person to follow through on commitments?
- *Self-Awareness:* Does he/she like herself/himself and seem to know herself/himself well? Is he/she emotionally balanced and open to personal growth or personal development?
- *Inspiration:* Is this person inspiring to you? After spending time with him/her, are you excited to see the person again? Can you imagine this person as your spouse? As a parent?

NOTE: Suggestions such as these are not designed to make the space "heavy." When dating for marriage you are standing in a place of being clear about your vision and your future and really having meaningful conversations. Someone asked me, "What if you go for drinks after work to a bar and someone approaches you; what do you say? Are you going to blurt out that you are marriage-minded?" Of course not, you'll just be you—the you who is committed to getting married as a life goal—comfortable in your skin with a clear vision. Through this dating-for-marriage process, you avoid wasting time with the wrong people.

Regardless of how and where you meet someone, just be yourself, and live your life powerfully. In this way, you'll be comfortable in any situation with tools to know when someone may be right for you.

Meeting Michael

*A successful marriage requires falling in love
many times, always with the same person.*

—Mignon McLaughlin

It was an ordinary Friday afternoon, and I was at the office running my recruiting company, BreakthroughIT. I was in the midst of some pretty regular dating, going on three coffee dates a week, and I participated in other dating-related activities for four hours a week. I had thirty minutes of free time, and I decided to spend it sorting through profiles on a dating site. I came across one that was unique: a handsome, forty-year-old with a few pictures of himself on a sailboat. From viewing his profile, I thought he was attractive, funny, obviously smart, and living life. It was a starting point.

He was one of only a few people who I e-mailed. I learned to navigate the dating sites with a fine-tooth comb, carefully screening for matching profiles, assessing a person as best as I could before meeting in person. I learned how to read between the lines (given the surface and limited questions asked on the dating sites) to extract what I could. If I felt we had matching ideals or values after a few e-mails and several phone calls, I would arrange a short coffee date. I learned to be proactive and have a positive, lighthearted approach while screening them for myself. A recruiter by nature, I knew the important questions to ask, because on the surface, you cannot necessarily assess a match.

When I first started dating, I received e-mails from many

wrong people I chose not to meet. Some of the funny (and some-times ridiculous) red flags included:

- Couldn't meet until 10:00 PM because they were busy.
- Suggested going to his place to watch a movie for a first date.
- Couldn't articulate goals.
- Self-absorbed.
- Talked about previous relationships in the first five minutes.
- Boring, negative, cynical, complaining, not marriage-minded, or just wrong, wrong, wrong.

So instead of waiting for men to contact me, I was proactive and was in the driver's seat of my life and my time. I decided that I was the prize and should treat myself as such for a change. Michael e-mailed back. We spoke on the phone in the morning and agreed to meet that afternoon—we decided to play it by ear and speak at 4:00 PM. I was fine with being flexible as I already had plans for later that evening, and spontaneity worked for me at certain times. We spoke at 4:00 PM and agreed to meet at a café across the street from the beach an hour later.

On the phone, Michael sounded like a busy, entrepreneurial guy who was up to things. I arrived at 5:00 PM, sat outside, admiring the ocean view while I waited. By 5:15, he hadn't yet arrived so I decided to wait just a few more minutes, then got up to leave. I called his cell phone to check, and it went to voicemail. No big deal—I had plans and wasn't particularly committed to any one date, so off I went. I didn't live by "the rules," but instead did what felt right to me.

I was about two blocks away when my cell phone rang: "Bari, they told me you were here and left! I'm so sorry for being late—I'm working on a big project and didn't allow enough time! Can you come back?" Since I was pretty curious about Michael and was very close by, I made a U-turn. There he was: curly black hair, olive skin, and very cute—a George Clooney in cowboy boots.

We waved to each other, and he hopped into my car to accompany me while I parked. From the first moment, he was warm and considerate . . . and exceptionally sweet. We drove one block, and I parked my car next to his at the Marriott where he knew the valet. I thought about how our shiny black cars could get to know each other as well.

Walking back to the café, we started to talk. The conversation was amazing and just flowed. He talked about his life and his love of sailing, his family, his business, and his passions. He described how he felt with the wind in his hair and what it was like to be on the water. He talked about architecture, his company, and his dad. We discussed travels and adventures—it was lighthearted and sweet. Both originally from New York, Jewish (with little Jewish background growing up) culturally, we meshed. On this date and our subsequent dates, we discussed the type of lifestyle we envisioned. We both had long, disappointing dating and relationship histories, and disappointments in how those previous relationships turned out.

Some important issues surfaced, like the fact that we both

valued partnership in a marriage very deeply. We discussed wanting a spousal relationship of working together and building a life and a business. In the past, we both didn't have that. We discussed family values; since I didn't yet have children, that was important to me. We shared very important ideals about creating a future.

He was very different from any of my other dates. He listened intently, and there was a feeling of comfort. When Michael shared certain ideas, I could feel the emotion in his eyes; they almost teared up. Time just flew during this great conversation, and before I knew it, I was lost in his energy. However, it was definitely time to leave. I still had plans that evening to attend a singles dinner in Miami, and I needed to get ready.

I already knew he was different. From our very first date (and all of our subsequent dates), Michael took care of me in a different way, because our personalities and goals meshed. It was like finding myself. He addressed my top emotional needs without knowing it, because it was simply natural for him to be authentic and warm, I could tell he was made of good stuff. It was clear: this man is real, not egotistical.

At the end of the date, he took my hand so gently, walked me back to my car, gave me a soft kiss on the cheek, and said he would like to see me again. He asked if I was free on Sunday night—not the common, "I'll call you" or the awful "I'll be in touch."

As I mentioned earlier, my most important emotional need is to be cherished, and by how he treated me, how the conversation went, his openness and expressiveness on that date (and on all subsequent dates), I felt in my core that he met that need. His character was unlike anyone I'd ever met, and our values and vision aligned as was revealed through our meaningful conversations as time went on. He was open and had a tremendous capacity for listening and sharing himself. He was different, different for me, and he was exactly what I needed.

When it's right, it will flow . . . and that's exactly what it did.

Have a Breakthrough! Create your Marriage Vision. Take some time to begin creating your vision.

My Top 5 Emotional Needs Worksheet page 165
My Values Worksheet page 169
My Personality Worksheet page 170
Life Goals Exercise page 174
My Marriage Vision Summary page 176

Date to Marry Tip: When it's right, you'll know.

At that perfect time, you'll have that "where have you been all of my life?" feeling. It really happens. When it's right, it just flows, as most happily married couples will tell you. Don't be overly concerned with questions like "How will I know if it's right?" I always assure the people I coach that, with the right person, it will be natural and effortless. Vision, values, and goals will line up and you will know. Truly.

Part III

ACT
in the Present:
Dating for Marriage
in Action

The Meet To Marry Coaching Program

The program is comprised of three parts: Assess—Attract—Act to get you "being" the one and fully ready and engaged in dating for marriage.

ASSESS Your Readiness
What does it truly mean to "be" the one to find the one? Access your readiness, uncover any blockages or blind spots related to dating, and embrace your own uniqueness.

Marriage Readiness Quiz	**Reality Check**	**Challenge Your Thinking**
Take this 10-point quiz to find out if you are truly ready to welcome your dream partner into your life now!	Have a breakthrough in seeing your current reality with a fresh perspective and create new empowering possibilities.	Do this exercise anytime to transform disempowering feelings into empowering facts.

ATTRACT Your Ideal Spouse
Attain clarity about your unique wants and needs in a relationship by using these tools to visualize and articulate your vision.

My Happiness Journal	**Dream Board**	**Marriage Vision**
Imagine it's already happened! Clarify your vision to attract your ideal spouse into your life.	Use this display as a tool to visual your dreams and realize them (and have fun in the process).	Articulate your: • Emotional needs • Values • Goals • Personality

ACT in the Present
Be in action consistent with your vision by dating for marriage using a principled approach.

Commitment to Success & Dating Plan of Action	**Dating Toolkit**	**Innovative Dating Tips & Slogans**
Make a commitment! Go for success by dating with structure. Date with a plan and fill your calendar with SMART goals to keep you motivated, positive, and organized.	Be empowered and confident when dating for marriage with the philosophy, steps, how-to's, and the most commonly asked questions about dating for marriage.	Practical tips, wisdom, and coaching to support you on your dating journey of "being" the one to find the one for you!

8

Align Your Actions with Your Dreams

Get leverage to create personal change by
associating an old behavior with massive pain, and
the desired new behavior with massive pleasure;
and when you get stuck, interrupt your limiting pattern
by doing something totally unexpected.

—Anthony Robbins

Hollywood producer Brian Grazer, known for more than fifty films, television series, and collaborations with Ron Howard, mentions in his essay, "Disrupting My

Comfort Zone," "If you're not growing, you are dying." To reach your goals, take an honest look at yourself and determine: "Am I doing what I need to do in order to move forward and achieve the goals and dreams I set for myself?" If not, then identify where you're out of alignment and what's holding you back, and then identify and take actions that are consistent with your dream.

There's a popular saying that goes something like this: "The definition of insanity is doing the same thing over and over and expecting different results." If you're still single, but you want to find and marry "the one," your pattern of action hasn't worked. In other words, you need to *leave your comfort zone and embark on a new reality.*

A new approach to dating starts by evaluating your beliefs and vision differently—especially those concerning yourself, others, and the nature of love and marriage—and then by moving into action based upon your newly clarified beliefs and vision in order to manifest your most fulfilling love life.

Seth Godin, in "Quieting the Lizard Brain" in *Linchpin*, asks, "How can I explain the never-ending irrationality of human behavior? We say we want one thing, and then we do another. We say we want to be successful, but we sabotage the job interview. We say we want to be thin, but we eat too much. We say we want to be smart, but we skip class or don't read that book the boss lent us."

We say we want to get married, but then we don't make dating a priority. We allow ourselves to be negative and cynical. We make excuses. We think no one is good enough.

Don't allow negativity, skepticism, or fear to prevent you from living an outstanding life. I learned to become my own best friend by giving myself a break and getting off of my back, loving myself, getting to know and believe in myself, and by doing self-promoting actions. I learned to recognize when my thinking was off-kilter.

At first, it happened very slowly. If I had a thought or a feeling that might be self-defeating or fear-based, I would challenge its validity, using the Challenge Your Thinking exercise (page 108), and then "squash it." Basically, I would ask myself, "Is that feeling real? Is that true?" and replace the thought or feeling with something more in line with reality.

There's a little voice inside of all of our heads that is constantly talking to us. That little voice is always voting, judging, and telling us what to do and what not to do. You might be thinking right now that this doesn't apply to you, but it's likely your little voice is saying, "What is she talking about?" Yes, that's the little voice I'm speaking about. It's the voice that says, "It's really scary out there. . . ." It's the voice that says, "Who will listen to what I have to say anyhow?" and what I said to myself: *You've made poor relationship choices for most of your life. . . . Why do think it will change?*

The good news is that this little voice can be trained. This little voice can be a messenger of fear, hurt, and shame, keeping you down and very far from your dreams, or it can be a messenger of hope, courage, pride, and determination, cheering you on to your life's mission. It's your voice—*you* get to train it.

An acquaintance asked my husband to contact an old friend he hadn't been in touch with in more than twenty years in order to inquire if her brother was single. She didn't know anything about the guy, except where he lived and that he looked handsome in a photograph she'd seen. This acquaintance, I'll call her Jill, heard about *Meet to Marry* and offered to tell all of her friends since "they needed it."

"What about you? Aren't you single?" I asked.

She responded that she is single. At thirty-nine, Jill is attractive and in action, and I asked her why she thought she was still single. She told me that she was "different" than most singles. She was looking for "someone exquisite." Yes, Jill used those words precisely. She explained that she needed a certain kind of guy who was exceptional (like her), and that what she wanted is very hard to find. No doubt. What she wanted was perhaps impossible, because no one would ever be good enough. *That is her blind spot and her little voice in action.*

After dating for more than fifteen years, she perceived herself to be so exquisite and exceptional that she completely disconnected from reality. It doesn't take a Ph.D. to see her protection mechanism and blind spot alive and well. Her inner voice, discussed above, was telling her that she is above it all and is "too good" for anyone. No one, yet, was "exquisite" enough for her and it's likely no one will be—unless she interrupts her thought process.

We are guided by and are convinced that our thoughts and feelings *are* the "the truth." But our thoughts and feelings are not the truth. The truth is the truth, and as I became aware that I had the capacity to challenge my beliefs and my thinking, my life was transformed. I made a commitment to notice thoughts and my patterns. On a day-to-day basis, I took on the willingness to grow and change, and so my life changed as a result. It's a day-by-day, sometimes hour-by-hour, or minute-by-minute commitment to developing a new you. But if *I* could do it, *you* can do it.

If Jill could see herself in a more realistic light and drop the list of unattainable, unarticulated expectations of "he must be exquisite" and allow herself to be real, she would find real love. Instead, she puts herself high on an unreachable pedestal, complete with unrealistic expectations.

Every person is special, "exquisite," and unique in his/her own way, and we *all* deserve happiness and love. Make a commitment to yourself to succeed, even if at first it's uncomfortable and strange—even if the scared inner voice in your head tells you to run for the hills. Tell your voice, "Thanks for sharing," and get into action. I made this commitment and performed the necessary actions you'll read about in the next section. . . and my life immediately started to change, and so will yours.

Commitment to Success

Ask yourself: How am I going to live today in order to create the tomorrow I am committed to? Leave your comfort zone and embark on a new reality. Make a commitment to your success. Make a commitment to yourself and your life to do things a little bit differently than you did before. Have faith that with new actions and a strong belief in yourself, you will achieve your dreams. Try it out and remember: you can always go back to the way you were. Your old ways will still be there. Feelings change, but commitments don't.

I AGREE to forgive myself and others in areas where I am holding on to regrets from the past. I agree to have compassion for myself and others and to realize that the past was part of my journey.

I AGREE to be open to this new dating philosophy, which might be contrary to advice I have received in the past.

I AGREE to "try it out" with the knowledge that I can always go back to the way I was dating before.

I AGREE to fill in *My Happiness & Finding My Life Partner Journal,* which will assist me in creating my Marriage Vision.

I AGREE to follow the *Dating Plan of Action,* which can lead me toward having what I want in my life.

I AGREE to use the Slogans and Date to Marry Tips to support me in my dating for marriage journey.

Dating Plan of Action

Since dating is a numbers game, it's the perfect time to jump-start your dating life—do it by making dating and dating-related activities a priority. You need a Dating Plan of Action that is consistent with your vision. Date with a plan? Yes, dating must be consistent and frequent. If you don't know where you're going, how can you get there?

Once again, we'll begin with the end in mind. Refer back to

the date you decided you would be married by (the date you wrote in your journal). Now, picture yourself standing at that point in the future (as though it's happened already), and then imagine looking back.

In the Dating Plan of Action (page 202), you will choose the action steps you will take (with a series of promises and commitments) to arrive at your goal. Have your calendar in front of you as you fill it in. You will fill in blocks of time as you go. Be sure to put forth your best effort and your clearest intentions. Each action step will keep you excited, busy, and acting consistently to find your life partner. By being busy and happy and having a schedule filled with great events and actions every week, you will become even happier and see results that much faster.

Each day, each step, each action should be planned to lift you up and bring you closer to your goal. I live by this motto: "Feelings change, but commitments don't." It means that if you plan to do something, it's best to stick with the plan and follow through even if you don't feel like it because your dream is bigger and stronger than any negative voice in your head. As Steve Allen points out in his best-selling book *Getting Things Done*, remembering your "why" and the ultimate purpose of the plan (to ultimately find your life partner) will not only keep you motivated and clarify your sharpness of vision, it opens up creative thinking about wider possibilities.[29]

---

29 Steve Allen, *Getting Things Done: The Art of Stress-free Productivity*. New York: Penguin, 2002, p. 65.

SMART Goals

Create your plan using SMART Goals. The acronym for SMART can be used to provide a more comprehensive definition for goal setting:

S = specific

M = measurable

A = achievable

R = realistic

T = tangible

The dating-related actions include: attending functions, networking, e-mails, phone calls, coffee dates, and online and offline dating. These are all great ways of meeting people and getting out there. Brainstorm to expand your vision of the possibilities, and remember to think outside of the box.

Social Functions: Do research to identify local singles (preferable) and nonsingles events (since nonsingles know singles) and activities you could attend. These could be lectures, wine tastings, book signings, parties, career networking events, speed dating, events at your place of worship, music concerts, poetry slams, art gallery openings, late-night museum socials, sporting events, and more. What events would be interesting to you that open-minded people would attend? Check local listings regularly for events that would be fun and meaningful to you. Find as many as possible and add them to your calendar.

Networking: Make a list of friends who have great marriages who can assist in recommending and introducing you to other singles. It is these people you will "train" to be your matchmaker. Think of other people who may know or spend time with singles.

Dating Sites: If you are a member of a dating site, how active have you been? Do you e-mail people or wait for them to e-mail you? Get proactive. Learn to read profiles with a critical eye for marriage-mindedness. Identify desirable personality traits, values, and goals. You are looking for people who seem sincere, have matching values, and are involved in life, as well as any other characteristics that would inspire you based on your vision.

Identify the amount of time every week that you want to devote to dating-related activities. For example, if you decide to set aside four hours every week, you could hypothetically break that up into attending one short function, one big event, sending out a few e-mails on the dating site, and going on one coffee date. What events will you attend?

Teach Others to Be Your Matchmaker

Given the fact that your family and friends care about you, they're naturally going to want to help by setting you up with other "nice" singles. But without intervention, you know the story: the short people are matched up with short people, and the scientists with the scientists, and you often end up going on dates that make no sense. Let's stop wasting time and add intelligence to the process.

First, make a list of everyone you can think of who you respect and admire because they have a great marriage or a big social/

professional circle. Contact them to let them know you would be very open to introductions based on specific parameters.

Use your My Marriage Vision Summary form (from Chapter 7) to share with others the kind of person you are looking for. The form includes your vision, values, and goals; your friends can ask questions to see if the match could be a good potential.

Have a Breakthrough:
Your Dating Plan of Action

Make a Plan:

Now that you have a positive mindset and clarity of vision, it's time to create a game plan as you would with any project. The plan will use the SMART goal approach as discussed earlier in this chapter—specific, measurable, attainable, realistic, and timely.

Dating Plan of Action

Be sure to have your calendar near you so you can fill in blocks of time and scheduled activities. Break up activities into categories and enter them into your calendar (i.e., browsing profiles, sending e-mails, networking, attending lectures, etc.).

I will spend _____ hours per week on dating-related activities.

I will spend _____ hours searching online.

I will send _____ e-mails to people whose profiles match what I am looking for (i.e., someone with character traits I like, someone

I might admire or would want to be like, someone with a common vision, similar goals, values, etc.).

I will go on _____ dates every week (i.e., in-person coffee dates, phone calls, video chats, etc.).

I will contact _____ friends and family members to see if they know any marriage-minded singles.

I will attend _____ events every month where there will be opportunities to meet new people who may be interesting and single (i.e., lectures, music events, cultural events, singles events, gallery openings, poetry readings, sporting events, etc.).

What events will you attend this week? (Do this weekly, entering activities into your calendar).

_____   _____

_____   _____

_____   _____

_____   _____

_____   _____

_____   _____

_____   _____

Tips for Dating to Marry

Since this chapter is about Dating in Action, the remaining tips and slogans follow. The tips below are tried-and-true, success-oriented action steps you can use while dating for marriage. In addition to being "tips," they are distinctions that I used every step of the way, and because the actions are principle-based, they go hand in hand with all areas of the program.

Date to Marry Tip: Make dating a priority.

If finding your future partner is important to you, don't hide out and pretend it's not that important. Chances are it won't just "happen," like in the movies. Make a plan and make it a priority! Sure, you could get lucky and meet him or her randomly. But as I mentioned, I was more likely to get struck by lightning twice than to just luck out and meet the right one without being in action.

Date to Marry Tip: Be your best, feel your best!
Love how you look and how you feel.

Take an objective look at yourself or grab a friend who will be honest and objective with you. There's nothing like a kind-hearted, yet genuine dose of "reality-based" feedback. Looking at your appearance and how you feel about it now will inspire you to step forward into a world of what's possible. Feeling great and having a great attitude is the surest way to boost your self-confidence. Since you've worked on being positive inside, it's the perfect time to take a look at your outside.

What would it take for you to increase your personal confidence to the next level? When you take that good look at your "whole picture," is there anything that you would like to enhance so as to feel and be at your best?

For both sexes, it's important to look at wardrobe and personal grooming. A new level of personal image and self-care, such as a weekly manicure, facial, and new hairstyle will make you feel wonderful about yourself. I personally made several changes in this area. The changes that were suggested to me were that I become more sensuous, wear more skirts and dresses, and to add some color to my cheeks.

My first reaction was that this so-called "feedback" wasn't necessary. I thought I looked fine. Then I realized that my makeup skills were lacking, and the last time I had paid much attention to any of it was in the late 1990s. I warmed up to the idea that I could have some fun with pampering myself, and it worked. Refining my feminine attributes could really increase my self-confidence, another blind spot of mine.

My nails were slightly bitten, my cheeks pale, and my wardrobe way too casual. With this new perspective and motivation, I made an appointment at a nearby salon and decided it was time to take a fresh look at my hair, nails, makeup, and wardrobe. I straightened my high-maintenance curly hair, started getting weekly manicures, and took makeup lessons at both MAC and Bobbi Brown cosmetics. I arranged for a monthly facial treatment and then went shopping for some new outfits.

With my amazing, long-overdue new look, I felt unstoppable! With only a few small changes, my confidence was through the roof. I had no idea how powerful taking these few action steps would be. A crucial blind spot was that I thought I looked really fine. Of course, in reality, there wasn't anything wrong with how I looked, but by paying attention to some new areas of appearance, *wow*! It was *exhilarating*. Before my makeover, I paid attention mostly to my business, and I didn't allow myself time for this type of pampering. Believe me when I tell you: *I'm so glad I finally did.*

Exercise: Be Your Best and Feel Your Best

What changes could you make to feel amazing about yourself? These could be as simple as an updated hairstyle or a few new outfits. Write these down in the form of "action items." Then, include them in your journal. Choose at least two action items drawn from your responses to the above question and schedule them into your calendar. Invite a friend to join you, if you like, and have some fun together!

I will take the following actions to feel, think, and be my best:

Action Item No. 1: _____

Action Item No. 2: _____

What further actions will you take? State your commitment out loud every morning (and more often, as necessary): "I will take the following actions and be loyal to the plan I make."

Use displays to support you. Create the Meet to Marry Dream Board, where you can paste photos, pictures, quotes, or anything really, that will inspire you on your journey.

How do you think you will feel after following through on your commitment to yourself and your plan?

Date to Marry Tip: Be 100 percent free of "attachments" to past relationships.

Attachment to old boyfriends, former dates, and former spouses will clog you up energetically, and will not leave room for "the one." When dating for marriage, you have committed to looking for your future spouse. At this time, it is better to surround yourself with friends of the same gender. Cut the ties to the past and see how good the results can be. If you ever find yourself romanticizing about the past, having regrets or even the occasional thinking about past "what ifs" this is for you. Note: If you have children from previous relationships, you obviously will have a connection to your former spouse. This tip refers in your case to cutting "emotional" ties (or regrets) that may hold you back from moving on.

Closure with Your "Ex"

Closure with past relationships is critical. You may find much resistance within yourself, but its achievement produces tremendous results. It is virtually impossible to move forward without it. I had an ex with whom I had been entangled for some time. The relationship had been over for many years, but for various reasons, we kept hanging on as friends. There was something incomplete in our now-ended relationship. Seemingly harmless entanglements like these kept both of us from moving on, in no uncertain terms. Remaining "friends" kept my energy like a clogged pipe; there was no hope for new love, so I needed to cut the ties completely. It was only by saying a definite good-bye that it would be possible for us to move on. I needed to have courage to persevere and not hang on. While this might seem like a very obvious and simple task for most, for me, it was like being disconnected from life support.

I chose a day to make the phone call and said good-bye. At the end of the day, he was pretty relieved. Cutting the cord did in fact allow us both to move on—and move on we did. He met someone soon after and got married, and I was on the road to finding Michael.

What past relationships are *you* holding onto?

➤ Releasing "Old Stories" ◀

Holding on to old loves, hurts, and childhood wounds:	Letting go and freeing yourself from the past:
• Carrying emotional baggage	• Possessing the wisdom to challenge unhealthy thinking
• Feeling sadness and regret (the shoulds and woulds plague you)	• Living in reality, content and balanced. Open-minded and authentic
• Remaining stuck in undesirable situations	• Being able to nake powerful, positive and empowering choices
• Feeling negativity, cyncism, blame, and frustration	• Being able to be forgiving and to see the good in all situations, (silver linings) and create positive outcomes
• Feeling powerless, overwhelmed, and fearful	• Feeling confident, self-assured, self-accepting, positive and optimistic
• Having low and clogged energy	• Being open, balanced, nonjudgmental with freedom to live life on life's terms

Date to Marry Tip: Remember that chemistry is important, but it's not the whole story.

We all know that attraction usually happens in a first glance. Relationships need fire; however, they can't thrive on chemical attraction alone—the jittery, heart-throbbing sort of attraction is not a requirement. What is important is to find someone with whom you feel a "spark" or chemistry. Chemistry is either there or it isn't. Although some sort of spark must exist, a relationship that is based purely on passion and physical attraction will rarely stand the test of time.

Common values, mutual respect and admiration, shared experiences, and empathy are qualities that typically ensure a relationship's endurance. Both physical attraction and shared values are essential to the development of a lifelong connection. After all, you don't want to marry a fiery obsession, and you also don't want to marry someone who is like a brother or sister.

Date to Marry Tip: Don't be friends with the opposite sex while dating for marriage.

The energy of a male and a female is, by nature, intimate, and while dating for marriage, it's best not to be friends with people of the opposite gender. While you might be skeptical, if you take it on, you will see that it's true. I did.

I expect your inner voice may be thinking that this sounds ridiculous or unreasonable. However, when examined more closely, it made sense to me, and it will for you too, as it has for countless skeptical singles who took it on.

Here is the gist: if you were to interview singles in urban centers with large dating pools, what are their chief complaints? *Everyone knows everyone, and everyone is friends with everyone else. It's familiar and painfully boring—all the same faces. I'm sure it would be better if I moved or lived someplace else.*

Since everyone is familiar, and men and women hang out as friends, there is an almost clanlike feeling—no mystery. When singles are all "friends" with each other, their secrets, vulnerabilities, and allure disappear.

Let me ask you this: Would you present yourself on a date the same way you would hanging around the house with your siblings or best friend? Would you discuss intimate dating concerns with people who couldn't understand you, who didn't have your best interests in mind, or worse, who view your vulnerabilities lightly? Of course you wouldn't. Friendship is intimate and knowing. It's safe and warm, brotherly or sisterly. Can "friends" who share this kind of intimacy view each other as potential spouses? Not likely. This is a *big* blind-spot area.

One woman I coached, who had "tons of guy friends," hung out with them because "it was harmless." But is it really harmless? While she laughed it off as not affecting her, she realized that some aspects of their friendship did bother her: their opinions and philosophies about dating were diametrically opposed to hers. She often listened "harmlessly" to her male friends openly reporting on their sexual exploits (since they were obviously not dating for marriage). She couldn't see previously that this was not a healthy space for her to be in. This is true for both genders when dating for marriage.

Many of us have read *Men Are from Mars, Women Are from Venus* by John Gray. Men and women *are* different. We would all agree that there are things that men discuss with men, and women discuss with women. One woman with an abundance of male friends (who didn't want to give them up) explained that of course there were certain things she wouldn't discuss with her guy friends. Of course there was a certain way she would never dress around them. Why? Because they are guys! With the opposite sex, there is still a level of intimacy—even just with friends.

Date to Marry Tip: "Coffee dates" for the first meeting; you can always meet again.

Avoid dinner, drinks, or the movies on the first date. After you've e-mailed a few times, spoken on the phone some, and feel inspired and confident that the person is both marriage-minded and has similar values and goals, then you can begin to explore further with a first "coffee date." As you're exploring to see if there's a spark, be sure this first date is in a public place conducive for conversation. How will you know if he/she is marriage-minded? Ask questions:

- What are your goals?
- What are you up to in your life?
- What are some of your core values?
- What is your vision for the future?

It's important that both parties verbalize their goals. As you ask them questions, also talk about your goals and values openly. Remember, one way you will know if someone is marriage-minded is simply because they say so. You're obviously not asking if the person wants to marry you, but we want to know if marriage is a life goal for them.

Examples of ways to tell him/her that you're marriage-minded include explaining confidently where you are in life:

> I'm happy to say that I know myself well. I have an M.A. in Communications, I've traveled to Europe and Thailand, and I practice yoga. I'm at the point where I'm ready to share my life with someone.

From the first conversations, share who you are and what you are about:

> I'm thirty-two years old, and I'm marriage-minded. I'm very excited about my life, and I'm dating to find the person I will share my life with.

When you're open about your intentions, it's empowering. If you try it this way, and your date is either scared off, turned off, or not ready, he/she is not in the same place as you. The good news is that you haven't wasted your time pursuing a relationship with someone who is obviously not the right match for you.

Date to Marry Tip: Conversation makes up for time.

Talking and getting to know each other, if done properly, can make up for time (even years) spent in long, drawn-out, "old paradigm" movie dates. Movie dates with little meaningful conversation shed little light on anything important. When dating for marriage, it's not important to fuss about how long to date. Every date should be in a setting conducive for an extended private conversation, and you'll both be candidly discussing your visions, core values, family goals, and other important issues related to life-building (while enjoying each other's company).

When Michael and I dated, we talked nonstop about life, our passions, our goals and dreams, as well as our failures. The experience was moving and exciting, and we knew then that it was right. Having meaningful conversations saves time you would otherwise be spending on dozens more dinner and movie dates. A woman shared with me that she and her husband went on ten long dates before they got engaged and had meaningful conversations each time. They've been married ten years, and she said that to this day, his character has never surprised her.

Given her example, it's clear that one way you can tell someone's depth of personality and character in ten dates is by talking, talking, and more talking about important issues. Did she know his third-grade math teacher? No. Did she know his favorite food when he was five or his favorite pizza topping? Of course not. However, these things are not things that she needed to know.

For some people, it will be clear in ten dates. For others, it may take longer. It's very individualized. Within six months of sharing experiences, you will have an excellent sense of who you're with. Six months' time together will ensure that what you see is indeed what you're going to get.

Slogans to Live By

Slogans are inspiring tools to propel you into positivity and motivation to create your new reality.

- Act in the present to secure the future.

- There's no future in the past.

- Reality—don't leave home without it.

- How will you know? It will flow.

- Never marry "potential."

- Be a mother/father to yourself. How can you expect others to love you if you don't love yourself?

- Live life on life's terms.

- Bad love is not better than no love.

Be your own coach (the observer inside of you), and challenge your unhealthy thinking.

- Fear (f. e. a. r.) is "false evidence appearing real."

- You attract what you send out.

- To thine own self be true.

- I lived, I loved, I learned.

- The only stable thing you can count on about life is that it will change.

- Don't go against the flow of life.

- If you're in your comfort zone, you're moving backward.

- If you don't want to be in the same place next year, or three years or five years from now, get into action.

- There is no growth without pain.

- Live life consciously.

- Attachment is the enemy of happiness.

- Your thoughts and your feelings are energy. Make sure they are positive: the universe is listening.

Have a Breakthrough

Put the Tips and Slogans to action in your life. Choose a tip and a slogan each week and see how it can impact you and your dating life.

Date to Marry Tip: Maintain physical boundaries until there is caring and commitment.

Your body is sacred, so why share it with someone you barely know? Since you are dating to marry, once you know it's right, there will be plenty of time.

9

Dating for Marriage Success

Our survival depends on the healing power of love,
intimacy and relationships. As individuals, as communities,
as a country, as a culture, perhaps even as a species.

—Dean Ornish

Now that you know the *Meet to Marry* concept of dating, I wanted to share several success stories that prove how these tried-and-true concepts worked in real life. The stories you will read about are stories of real people who lived this program and philosophy. There's an expression that there's no change without growth, and the people you'll read about know both sides. They weren't born into this dating system and philosophy but rather chose to embrace it in order to have a future not dictated by their past. In each case, the individuals made choices to *be* conscious singles, and the gift they received is the kind of spouse they only dreamed of.

Success Story: Jamie, on Dating for Marriage

Jamie received a master's degree from an Ivy League school when she decided to take a year off to learn, travel, and explore her roots. She was raised in a nonreligious family and lived the normal college life. Jamie had had a serious boyfriend for several years beforehand whom she was afraid to break up with (he was great on paper but didn't share her values). She shared her wisdom on the topic of marriage-minded dating with me. Her enthusiasm about the process was truly inspiring, confirming that there is indeed romance and miracles in discovering "the one" in this way.

    Bari: What was your dating like before you decided to date for marriage?

  Jamie: I would say typical American. In high school, I dated a lacrosse player. We would go out after school and on weekends.

    Bari: How long was that relationship?

  Jamie: About five months.

Bari: How long was your longest relationship?

Jamie: Three years, with a guy from college. I dated a couple of guys, one for two years, and one guy for three years, during college and after. I would say all those relationships were very typical American, college-style relationships.

Bari: Full service?

Jamie: Absolutely.

Bari: Let's fast-forward to how you're dating now. How does dating for marriage work? How do you meet people?

Jamie: Basically you talk to rabbis, matchmakers, and rebbetzins (wives of rabbis) and people who are well connected. They ask you about where you are in your life, what you want, what your goals are, what your perception of Judaism is, how you want to live your life, what things are very important to you, and what you are looking for in a mate. They also ask you about deal-breakers, where you want to live, and things like that. After you have a very in-depth meeting with them, they start to look through the people they know. Maybe they know guys in yeshiva (religious school), maybe they know guys from here or there. Somehow they think of someone they think sounds like what you want, and they tell you about them. If they sound good to you, then maybe you would talk on the phone. Once you talk on the phone, if that goes well, only then would you go out. You don't just meet people and go out with people who don't share the same things that you want. You only go out with people who you have already predetermined share all the important values with you. You're not wasting your time.

Bari: How did you come to dating like this? What happened to bring you to this situation?

Jamie: It started after that guy I dated in college for three years. He wasn't Jewish, and because I was becoming more interested in Judaism, my roots, and my heritage, we just grew more and more apart, as well as other things.

Bari: And you came to Israel, right?

Jamie: Yes, eventually. We broke up, and for about eight months I was single. I tried dating through a Jewish dating site, and I tried dating people in between, people who were not so religious, but who were at least Jewish. That wasn't right either. In every situation I was in, it was becoming really clear to me that it was not the right situation. Soon, I quit that, and I decided I really needed to come to Israel to figure out what I wanted in religion and Judaism before I continued to date. With the exception of one relationship, I didn't date for about two years.

Bari: So now you feel like you're marriage-ready. How old are you?

Jamie: I'm twenty-four.

Bari: Why do you feel like you're ready to be married now?

Jamie: First of all, I feel like I've really gotten to know myself, what I want, who I am, and what is important to me. I've done a lot of learning. I've grown professionally. I have my license and my master's, so career-wise, I know what I want and I'm moving in that direction. I spent time exploring myself, and I've worked a lot on an emotional level. Then I came to Israel. I've been here for more than six months, learning the Torah and Judaism. Now I've really been solidifying some of these spiritual values. I kind of feel like those three worlds are coming together: my professional, my emotional, and my spiritual lives, not to mention that twenty-four is a pretty normal age to get married. Most of my friends are getting married anyway, so it doesn't feel so early, for sure. It feels very normal, even in a religious society.

Bari: Your stated goal is to get married. Do the guys who you're being set up with have the same vision?

Jamie: Exactly, and I don't even meet them unless they already want what I want. I don't waste my time falling for guys before I figure out if it makes sense for me. I don't want to get hurt anymore and waste my time fooling around when you don't know where it might lead. Maybe you have major differences, and I don't want to waste time like that. One might say that it takes the romance out of it, but I really beg to differ because—

Bari: That was my next question. Is dating for marriage romantic?

Jamie: Yes! There is something far more romantic in looking for a husband and father of your children than someone who you happen to think is good-looking. It's so superficial—first you go for looks and *then* you get to who they are? In my situation, all the values come first, and then I consider their looks and whatnot. It's on a deeper level of connection and attraction, a much deeper level. Not to mention that the dating is a little bit faster because you already know so much about someone before you even first meet. Before your first meeting in a regular dating situation, you know what they look like and you may know what their job is, but that's basically it. You can try to interpret other things based on the way they're dressed, but you don't know anything that is very important about them.

Bari: It's superficial?

Jamie: Exactly.

We continued by discussing the process itself, and how the specifics of dating for marriage worked for her.

Bari: Tell me about a first phone call.

Jamie: The matchmaker [who is a teacher at her school] tells you things about them, like where they went to school, what they want, what they were studying, and what their philosophy is on a lot of things. On the phone, you might start from some of the things that you heard. Maybe we talk about which yeshiva he's studying at, what kind of philosophy that school has, and what he's learned from that. We also talk about how he grew up. It's very common to ask about family, where he's from, what it was like there. Those are common things.

Bari: What's a first date like?

Jamie: The first date was three hours long. We talked about family, about Judaism. We started off with more typical question-and-answer stuff. Later, it got to a point where we were actually talking about philosophy and other deep things. We progressed into talking about everything, all the important things. You don't spend a lot of time talking about favorite TV shows or different movies.

Bari: You've told me that there's someone you're interested in and that you're about to go on a fifth date. What are you excited about, since it's so fresh?

Jamie: I feel like I already know all the important things about him, so I feel that I know that we're completely in sync with our values. I'm not worried that we'll have big differences. If there were big issues between us, they would have come up by now, either in our conversations or through the matchmaker. We have a good time talking, hanging out together, and laughing.

Bari: What are the things you have in common that would make you good partners? You mentioned family backgrounds, education, what else?

Jamie: We come from very similar cultures, socioeconomic backgrounds, and we both reached the same educational level. Actually, with education, we have a lot in common. Both of his parents have master's degrees. Both of my parents have graduate degrees. He has a graduate degree in political science, and I have a graduate degree in social work. The fact that he's American is huge, because I can already assume a lot of commonality of culture. It's very understated, but the differences between even a South African or an Australian with an American can be huge. I guess being with an American makes me feel closer to home. As I am a *ba'al t'shuvah* (return to religion), the fact that he was raised in a more secular Jewish family and became more religious too, our path to Judaism is something we share. We talked about that a lot, on the phone, on our dates, and we realized that we both went through the same experience. We both became more religious, and as we're both very close with our families, neither of us wanted to offend them. We can very much empathize with how hard these transitions are, with eating kosher especially, and Shabbat, and not wanting to offend our parents. The fact that we can empathize and really relate to these difficult things is very important. We also had very similar college experiences, and we both learned about Judaism at the same time. Today we're both in the same place religiously. It's so rare, it's unbelievable. I've been looking for someone who is like me in this way. I feel we came from the same background, and now we're also both in the same place religiously. Our direction is the same. That is really *amazing*.

Bari: That *is* amazing.

Jamie: He's at the same place as I am religiously, and we both want to create a Torah-centered home for our children. I think those are all very important.

Just a few months ago, before her current marriage-minded dating and budding relationship, Jamie cried to me about the fact that her boyfriend back home didn't share her vision and goals. She thought she might have to sacrifice what she wanted to be with him. She would ask me, "Bari, what if I don't find someone else? How can I break up with him?"

Jamie's mother liked her boyfriend back then, really thought it would work out, and told her daughter to simply not worry. But Jamie *did* worry about it because her vision of a spiritual family observing Shabbat was not something her old boyfriend wanted—he had different values and goals. I explained that her mom, while coming from a good place, could only see the situation from her own frame of reference. Her mother wasn't in a place where she could advise her in this situation, since religious life was not on her radar. And Jamie's father wasn't Jewish himself.

> *Jamie:* I was so stupid.
>
> *Bari:* You weren't stupid, you were so human. In the end you went for what you wanted. I'm so proud.
>
> *Jamie:* I can't believe it, because you can't really be with someone when you have such a different view on something that is so important to you.

This is what Jamie had to say about "old" dating versus dating for marriage:

> *Bari:* What's the difference between dating before, the old way,

and dating now, the new way? What is it like to date for
marriage? You're not being physical, so tell me about that
and what that's like for you.

Jamie: Before this, I obviously was not *Shomer Negiah* (not touch-
ing people of the opposite sex). It's confusing because with
my old boyfriend I'm not actually sure if the relationship
would have survived as long as it did without sex. Is sex a
major thing that holds people together, like a glue? I really
don't know. I know you can't have a relationship based on
that. It's ridiculous. You have to have a relationship built
on a firm foundation like having the same values, compli-
mentary personalities, and chemistry. Those are far more
important.

Bari: And on a practical side, how does that work?

Jamie: Now, we just get to know each other. I feel like we have a
lot more clarity. First of all, you know that he's not interested in you just for that reason. He's not just interested in
you temporarily. He's not just interested in you physically.
He's thinking about you as his potential wife and mother
of his children. That's a completely different view.

Bari: People will totally be able to relate to that, because so
many women get hurt and stuck in these relationships,
and they confuse sex and love. Even men do.

Jamie: Yes, so much.

Bari: You were saying that your friends in the States—

Jamie: Yes, my friends living in New York are still dating secu-
larly, which would be fine, except that they are not happy.

If they were happy, then that's fine with me, but they're not happy. Mainly, I think it's because what most women want is to be in a stable, committed relationship with a man who loves them. What's happening is that many women out there are offering themselves physically without necessarily being in the relationship they want.

Jamie then went on to share a moving story she learned. It is a parable I'll call "The Diamonds Disguised as Tomatoes."

Jamie: I learned this parable about how all women are diamonds. That's our soul. All of us are shining diamonds. The problem: some women camouflage themselves as tomatoes. They actually put tomatoes on themselves and cover up their diamond soul within. They put themselves in such a low place, where they accept no commitment or little commitment, and receive bad treatment. And then they give up so much, just—maybe it's fun. It is fun, for the time being, to be in a physical relationship, but ultimately, I have seen that it doesn't make you happy in the long run.

There are two kinds of men. The first kind is a man who wants an easy tomato, a one-night stand, or he's looking for a girlfriend. What these men really want is fun. They're looking for the tomato girls. The problem is the tomato girl really wants to be with the diamond boy.

The second kind of man is looking for diamonds. These men can't see the diamond girl, because she's underneath the camouflage of a tomato. There are amazing guys out there—this isn't bashing men. These amazing guys who are looking for diamonds are not going to be attracted to you because you're camouflaging yourself as a tomato. All the while, there *are* girls out there who look like diamonds and treat themselves like diamonds. They won't put up with men who are interested in treating them however they want.

When my friends come to me and complain about how men treat them badly, I just tell them that they act and look like tomatoes. They don't show anyone that they're really diamonds. I know they're diamonds. My friends are all really beautiful women who basically want the same thing. They are *all* beautiful diamonds. When you act and treat yourself as a tomato, that's all the boys can see.

Bari: Why are they doing that?

Jamie: They think that it will make them happy, and, for the short term, it does. It is nice to have someone warm in your bed, and it is nice to get physical affection. It is nice. All of that is great. I'm not going to lie. I was there. I can testify that it all seems great at the time. But does it all lead to happiness? No. Does it lead to satisfaction? On some level, yes. You might have some sexual satisfaction, and you might have some emotional satisfaction. You might have some good times, and you might not be lonely. But really, are these women happy? I have not felt that my friends going through this are actually happy.

Bari: So these women are selling themselves out short-term.

Jamie: Yes, I always tell my friends that if you like a guy and you want a serious relationship, do not sleep with him. Keep physical boundaries. Number one, you're going to see whether he's actually a quality guy interested in you. Number two, you're going to find out whether you actually have feelings for him, and not get mixed up with all the physical things. Sex confuses women because emotions kick in and it's easy to mix up intimacy for genuine connection. *Nobody* is actually a tomato. It's just a cover-up. People can't see. Men don't have x-ray vision to see that you're really a great woman inside. I talked to a couple guys who are secular, and they've said it's very endearing, and they really respect it when a woman keeps boundaries. They respect that you treat yourself with such dignity. Having self-worth makes them want you more. I've talked to regular guys about this topic, and they think, "Wow, this is pretty cool, actually." They think that. However, I would be lying to say that what I've chosen is easy and fun all the time. It's a sensitive thing. It's very hard, and, of course, for somebody who came from that, you're used to it. Basically it's really hard to not even touch a guy for two years. I will be the last person to tell you that it is an easy transition. However, I believe that it will lead to so much greater happiness. But in the long run, once I'm married, I think that physical part will be even better. Nobody is going to say that it's easy to date someone without even brushing up next to them. I do believe that it will lead to much higher happiness.

Jamie was recently married in a lovely ceremony with all of her friends and family by her side. Throughout the dating process, she would tell me how wonderful her fiancé was. Everything was in alignment and the future was unfolding. She told me about their conversations about the future and how he proposed.

Jamie's story is a beautiful illustration of how she allowed herself to do things in a completely different way and got the life she wanted. Had she succumbed to the fear of "What if I don't meet someone else?" she would not have given herself the opportunity to have the life she dreamed of.

Jamie stepped out of her comfort zone in several ways. She trusted herself, and she trusted the process. She found mentors and listened to them. She decided to move forward in a principled way and had faith.

Dating for marriage is a new and different way of finding your life partner. If you don't go out on random dates based on attraction and interests, how do you do it? People want rules and solid answers, so I have included a "frequently asked questions" section later in this chapter. What's important to keep in mind is that when someone is marriage-ready, positive, and free of their baggage, the rules don't necessarily apply. Because a marriage-minded single is open and grounded, he/she trusts instincts rather than needing to follow strict rules.

Rules for dating are necessary *when the emphasis is external*. When you're marriage-ready, you'll know if you should see someone again. You'll respect your own boundaries. You'll feel free to communicate your needs and ask questions of the other. You'll have the clarity when you're dating. If someone you meet over coffee is nervous, but he's got all the qualities you are looking for, his/her nervousness may just be endearing to you. Remember, don't second-guess: *your gut never lies.*

A Dating for Marriage Success Story: Julie and Jacob

Julie (twenty-five) and Jacob (thirty-four) were recently married after having dated for marriage in the orthodox Jewish tradition described earlier. This is how they described that experience.

Bari: How did you meet Jacob?

Julie: A friend of mine told a rabbi about me. He knew Jacob, and they wanted to set us up.

Bari: Did you talk on the phone first? How did it work?

Julie: First, we researched each other and then spoke on the phone. It's a whole process. We sent our profile to the rabbi who knew Jacob. The profile had descriptions of ourselves, our goals, what it was that we wanted, descriptions of ourselves, and different references. Then we looked into each other. We either called those references or had other people call the references. Then we both decided that it sounded like we were on the same track. We went through the rabbi for the first few dates, and after that, we did it on our own. We felt more comfortable, and things progressed.

Jacob: Can I interject?

Bari: Please, I would love to hear your perspective.

Jacob: I was looking for a long, long time, for like six years, already. I read a lot of profiles and her profile spoke to me. In her profile, there were things in there that just sparked my interest. We came from similar backgrounds. Although there is an age difference, there were certain things that were uncannily similar. I felt so comfortable reading her profile; I was drawn in, even though I had never met her or saw a picture. I felt enthusiastic. At thirty-four, I felt a lot of pressure. People wondered, "What's wrong with this guy? Why is he not getting married?" You start to doubt yourself, naturally. The thing is, over time I've learned that people need to trust themselves. I grew so much when I started to listen to what I really wanted. I really trusted I was going to find the right person, and I'm glad it didn't work with the other women I had dated. I trusted my instincts enough to stick around for something amazing. It was worth the wait.

Bari: I definitely understand it was worth the wait! What I hear you saying is that in order to trust yourself, you have to know yourself and what you're looking for.

Jacob: Yes, I knew what I was looking for. In the profile, I saw that she had a South African background that was very interesting too. I could see our families would relate and that we would probably have a lot in common.

Bari: Would you say that the process is romantic?

Jacob: For me, this experience has been, yes, but it doesn't necessarily mean that it has to be. Should I elaborate?

Bari: Please.

Jacob: Love, for example, develops over time. Sometimes it happens straightaway, and that's an amazing experience. I'm a romantic, so I was hoping for that. It doesn't necessarily have to happen like that. When people have a feeling that "I'm in love with the person," it's not necessarily a real love. It's more like lust or more of something that is external. You can only love a person when you know the person. How can you know a person in such a short amount of time? Love can only come from seeing strength in the person, seeing how the person complements you, how the person lives their life. I'm not negating the fact that there can be a romantic relationship from the beginning.

Bari: What messages did you get growing up about marriage? How do you think that influenced you?

Jacob: My parents have a very good relationship with each other. My father is a very gentle guy and my mother is an *eishes chayil* (a woman of valor, a biblical reference and highest praise for a woman). They are nice people, and they have an unbelievable marriage. They're extremely generous and have people over to their house all the time. I would imagine that I picked that up from them. There are other influences that I've had along the way also. My parents, I would imagine, are the strongest. Again, that doesn't mean that somebody who didn't grow up in such a positive environment can't become an amazing husband or wife. I think people who have grown up in a negative environment can

> consciously decide to create their own home and family differently. There are no rules, really.

Julie: I want to add one thing about your romance question within this dating system. I think it's set up in such a way that there is a progression. Things don't happen all at once. In a more secular relationship, you can meet a person and "fall in love," and then it's over. This is because it's likely not a real thing. With how we did it, it typically can't happen so quickly. This system is set up in a way that you're encouraged to progress at a certain pace, which is the way real feelings develop, anyway. I think that it's all set up within the system. Does that make sense?

Bari: It makes total sense. If you're interested in marriage, don't look for love at first sight. We shouldn't look for a "television romance." We need to seek out something deep and authentic, to find someone who is right for you. And yes, love builds over time.

Jacob continued to tell me it's the whole person, the package, that's important, not any one external thing.

Jacob: The package is the personality: the external and internal and the background. The package is everything basically, and that's what makes a person attractive to you. Everything included. It's not just what you see on the outside. My attraction to Julie came from everything she is, the whole package. It's the family, it's her upbringing, and it's how she speaks, who she is. It's everything. It's her freckles. I like her freckles. Sure, I still doubted myself a lot, but I started with this important premise: to trust in God. You have to believe with certainty that in the right time God is going to send you your *bashert*, or marriage partner, or whatever definition you want to use. That faith has to be strong.

Bari: How did you know that Jacob was the one?

Julie: What a question! I think what Jacob was saying about the two of us just matching on both a practical and intellectual level is right on. Things just clicked with us. We had the same vision. Then, everything else was there. For me, it was very simple and quick. I just knew.

Bari: Do you have any advice for marriage-minded people beginning this journey?

Jacob: Be *b'simcha* (happy) that whatever situation you find yourself in, it's because that's the way God wants it to be, even though you don't see the ultimate result right now. Stay focused on your vision, so when you do meet the person you will be able to recognize that this person in front of you has the same goals, the same outlook on life, and is going in the same direction you're heading in. You've also got to make sure you have people you trust, that you can talk to, that can support you in making the right decision. No one can make the decision for you, but people can help you see if you are thinking along the right lines. Once you make the decision, everything fits into place. It's unbelievable. Everything really does fit into place.

Dating for Marriage Cheat Sheet

Keep in mind that you are not looking for a lot of second dates. You are looking for "the one." So keep these parameters in mind as you meet people online, through introductions, or at singles events.

1. Be your amazing self (free from blind spots and blockages by completing the Assess portion of the coaching in Chapters 1–4).
2. Create your My Happiness & Finding My Life Partner Journal and your Marriage Vision to clarify your vision for yourself of the type of person you'd like to marry based on the reality of who you are.
3. Use your Dating Plan of Action to get busy in your life to find sincere, marriage-minded singles. (Use your mentor, introductions, dating sites, singles events, etc.)
4. Screen people to assess:
    a. Is this person marriage-minded? (You will know by asking, "What are your life goals?")
    b. Assess if you share common vision, values, and goals
    c. Do you like this person's personality (Is he/she into things that inspire you?) Ask meaningful questions.
    d. Is this person inspiring to you?
5. If there seems to be potential via phone and e-mail, the first meeting should be a coffee date where you'll assess if there is attraction or a "click"; again, not a chemical or lusty attraction, but affinity and a click in conversation—a flow.

6. If many of the basics are yes, meet again; if not, remember you are not looking for a lot of second dates, you are looking for the one.

7. When strong potential exists, you will date this person and having meaningful conversations about the elements we've discussed on your dating journey with them to see if this person is the one.

8. When it's right, you will know.

Dating for Marriage: Frequently Asked Questions

Q. How will I establish that someone is marriage-minded?

A. *By having meaningful conversations. Let him/her know you are marriage-minded and excited about exploring conversations of real substance. If the person is not marriage-minded, better to know from the beginning. Talk about life goals and values as part of the discussion. Share your goals and ask about theirs in return. Ask about their plans for the future, and don't be afraid to share "who you are," not what you do. Profiles on dating sites can only reveal so much, so you'll need to ask a lot of questions before you meet. You are looking for someone with a personality you like. See if the conversation flows. If enough elements align, meet for coffee; if not, move on.*

Q. How will I know if I should meet someone in person?

A. *Before you meet someone in person, you need to establish that he or she is marriage-minded. Exchange a few e-mails and, if promising, speak on the phone first. Once you have established marriage-mindedness and have discussed basic elements of a match, then and only then should you meet for coffee.*

Q. How do I schedule a date?

A. *Since you've got a busy, active, happy life, you need to set the stage for the date. You don't want to put off meeting, so propose that you will simply meet for coffee to see if there's a connection. If there is attraction and a flow of conversation on this coffee date, you want to establish if there is a chance for something more. You also want to see if you like the person's personality, if he/she is into things you admire, and so on. Note: Chemistry is not the heart-throbbing, romantic, love-at-first-sight kind of attraction. It's more like attraction or affinity. You will know. If it's not there, it's not there.*

Q. How long should the first date be?

A. *First dates should be short coffee dates unless you have a more complete idea of the person's personality, values, and goals (from either a matchmaker, an introduction, or if you've had several phone conversations verifying the commonality). If you know more about the person, either because you've logged enough talking time on the phone, via video chat, or if the person will be flying in to meet you, that would be the only time to meet for longer than a coffee date. It's best to meet in a public place conducive to conversation.*

Q. How do I tell someone that I'm not interested in meeting again?

A. *Since your time and your date's time are valuable, it's critical to be clear. You can say, "I think you are a great person, but I don't see a match here. I really appreciate having met you." You can offer to tell them about a friend who may be a better fit. People appreciate honesty, so they don't waste their time either. No need for game playing. Always treat each date with the utmost respect, whether or not the person is for you. If you would like to see the person again, suggest a date and time to meet again. Dates should not be left open-ended.*

Q. Why do you suggest no second dates? What if I'm not sure?

A. *You will be sure. You will look for attraction (if affinity is there or not), a flow, and when someone "great" comes along, you will know it. Have faith. Second-guessing is a time-waster, especially if you are free and clear by having become marriage-ready. Trust yourself.*

Q. What about being physical and dating?

A. *I recommend not sleeping with anyone you are dating until you have a sense of mutual caring and emotional commitment. Physical relationships before commitment can lead to confusion and disappointment. By maintaining simple sexual boundaries, you will experience greater self-esteem and will be able to focus on getting to know a person in a meaningful way without distractions. When you are with the right person in the context of a committed relationship, you will have a lifetime of physical contact.*

Bari and Michael's Wedding

Our wedding was many years ago.
The celebration continues to this day.

—Gene Perret

Our wedding took place on a balmy day in late August on the hills outside of Jerusalem. We were on a ten-day trip to experience Israel by hiking, learning, and traveling. The country is so small yet so varied that in eight days it was possible to see its entire diversity of beaches, mountains, deserts, and plains. With my Nicole Miller dress in tow, we knew we would be getting married in Israel, but we still didn't know how it would unfold.

Given that we didn't know anyone there, and our touring schedule ran from 6:00 AM until after midnight each day, it didn't leave much time to make arrangements. Our guide's wife, Leah, offered to help us organize the wedding, and she suggested that we consider having it where they live, in Efrat, instead of our first choice, the holy and mystical city of Tzfat. Leah's generous offer to organize our wedding for us was one we couldn't refuse. She explained that school was still out for the last week of summer vacation, and people were free, and happy to participate in a wedding.

We would be having guests! We expected our wedding to be a simple spiritual service with just a rabbi and witnesses. Instead, we had more than fifty people, most of whom we met for the first time at our wedding. With our new friends as witnesses, we had the most intimate ceremony. In Hebrew, the word for such a happy event is a *simcha*, which means joy. That was precisely what our wedding was!

The generosity of the community was overwhelming. One couple invited me to get ready at their home, and someone else volunteered to do my makeup. Another person found a guitarist, and the photographer came after work. People stepped up to pick up my bouquet and even to bring the rings we'd chosen. There was a new caterer in town who was very happy for the business, even on such short notice. It all came together in four days! In the States, it could have taken a year to plan such an event. We were incredibly grateful and in awe of the spirit of these people.

The wedding was nothing short of a dream. Michael met with the rabbi and witnesses to sign the *ketubah* (marriage contract), while I finished getting ready. The location had been kept a secret from me, and when I was accompanied from the house to the chuppah (wedding canopy), it was clear how enchanted this moment was. The striking vista of the Judean hills spread endlessly before me. Michael, my future husband, and the waiting guests gathered around the splendidly decorated gazebo, and all were looking up toward me. The walk down the long path was surreal, more beautiful than a movie. *I felt like a queen.*

It was always my dream to have an Orthodox Jewish marriage ceremony, and ours exceeded my expectations. The sun set as I circled my future husband seven times.[30] With his arm around me, Michael took me under his *tallit* (prayer shawl). With holy ground under our feet, we recited the seven blessings. We broke the glass and everyone danced joyfully to Israeli music.

Hours later with me still in my wedding dress, we left the reception, which was held in a small synagogue, to catch our plane. People at the airport yelled *mazal tov* and *b'haztlacha* (congratulations and good luck), and in an instant we were on our way back to the States on an unbelievable high to see family and friends. With such a warm celebration, our future could not have been brighter.

I dreamed of a life of adventure with a guy with a huge heart and the capacity to love and give—and I got that. This is how our lives began. As I mentioned earlier, the wedding is only the

---

30 Under the chuppah, the custom is that the *kallah* (bride) circles the *chatan* (groom) seven times. Just as the world was built in seven days, the *kallah* is figuratively building the walls of the couple's new world together. The number seven also symbolizes the wholeness and completeness that they cannot attain separately.

beginning. This beautiful event was the foundation for our life together. It was the first day of the rest of our lives. Love does grow stronger and our bond tighter through our appreciation for each other and the life we continue to build together. I am profoundly grateful, and this is the joy I wish for you.

~~The end~~
The beginning

10

Create Your Future

You've read the Meet to Marry success stories and had a first-hand look at the coaching philosophy that has made a difference in the lives of so many people. Now, I want to leave you with a few things to think about as you move forward.

First, what are you going to do *starting right now* to Be the One? To create the life you dream of? To create a life of partnership with the full depth of connection you desire?

You've already learned so much from reading this book; I want to leave you with the reassurance that the Meet to Marry program is simple. But as I mentioned in the beginning, simple does not mean without commitment, awareness, and a shift in your thinking. The one common factor in every success story—my own and all the others I've seen—is the choice each individual makes to *be the one.* There is no how-to-get-everyone-to-love you chapter in this book. On the contrary, when you are *in love with yourself,* when you're balanced, grateful, and in reality, everything else falls into place. And believe me, that feeling is nothing short of miraculous!

When you choose to *be the one* in your life, the same harmony you find in yourself will radiate to all areas of your life, and eventually things will start to come together naturally, but only if you are open to choosing to see miracles. The miracles I am referring to occur in your everyday life and in the shift you make in choosing to see that every experience is designed for your personal growth for the positive. In every occurrence, you have choices to make in your attitude: for example, a supposed "bad date" can be viewed as negative, or it can be viewed as bringing you closer to the one. Little by little you can challenge your own "fakakta" thinking and transform it into healthy thinking. Believing really is seeing—so choose!

Choosing to *be the one* requires the willingness to look deeply and critically at your belief systems from the past and uncover your truth for yourself. When you eliminate those addictive shoulds, coulds, and woulds from your life, you'll be free to see the positive in everything that happens. One of the ways to access this freedom I describe is through gratitude and knowing that everything in your life is as it should be. What made a major difference for me was changing my lens and allowing life to just unfold. I learned that I had to stop trying to control people or forcing situations; I stopped beating myself up (got off of my own back) and began to appreciate my own humanity. By doing so, I no longer needed to attract the "wrong" men to support my old feeling of "something is wrong."

Once I experienced those miracles in my own life, I began sharing the program with other singles. I wanted to test all of it on singles of all ages and genders, on anyone who expressed interest in getting married but was having difficulty—the most skeptical and cynical, the most resistant to change, the never-married, the divorced, and singles who were serial daters.

What I found in all of them was that they allowed their pasts to dictate how they lived in the present. They all had a gap between what they said they wanted and who they were being. And through the coaching, by uncovering their blind spots, they all got to a place of choosing to *be the one* in their lives. They became happy, empowered daters who were comfortable in all situations and had clarity about the kind of person they would like to marry.

One of the most skeptical, negative, and closed people I coached (a fifty-three-year old woman who had never been married and who had extremely negative belief systems about men) said the following in her post-coaching feedback:

> The coaching pried open a tightly closed lid and let some optimis-

tic light to shine upon some long-held negative suppositions about dating and relationships. Many of the concepts are helpful in nudging my thinking and actions in a more positive direction.

Several months after the coaching, this client let me know that she is in a serious relationship! By uncovering her blind spot related to men and the origin of her "story," she become free. Not only has her dating life changed but her financial situation drastically changed as well. When you choose to *be the one*, life transforms—almost in spite of you. When I asked how her new relationship was going a few months after her breakthrough, here is what she said in an e-mail:

> He's coming over in a few minutes for a pancake breakfast. A couple of months ago, I gave him a serious list of all the reasons why he should start dating other people and avoid me like the plague. I told him to "Run fast, run far." He was undeterred. Eek!

As you move forward toward being the one and choosing to create your dream life, ask yourself these questions on an ongoing basis:

- What is about me that is keeping me stuck or unclear?
- What am I willing to do to let those things go and really experience life?
- When am I being my "old story" (i.e., phony or living in the past)?

I often ask those I coach, and now I ask you, "What is the price of holding onto *your* disempowering stories?" The answers vary, but they usually include answers like your humanity, your God-given uniqueness, your freedom of expression—your dreams!

The process of building new behaviors is just like building a muscle. When you are clear about who you are and what you are committed to, life just works. When you are being true to yourself, things begin to go your way and you meet the right one; circumstances align with your vision. You are no longer going against the flow of life.

Being the one also means asking questions with a beginner's mind. What is the reality of this situation? What is the truth for me? How is my attitude? Am I being free or fearful? Am I being my potential or my limitation? Am I being my old story or my new, empowering story? The answers to these questions will set you free to invent and create the life you dream of. When you become clear about who you are and what you want, you also become willing to say what's true for you. So whether you are searching on a dating site, interacting on a social network, receiving introductions, speed dating, or attending a singles event, your own wisdom will guide you—provided you are *being the one*.

Many have used this philosophy to realign their belief systems and achieve breakthroughs. This includes ordinary people like the thirty-nine-year-old woman you read about who was stuck on "I need someone exquisite" until she realized that her "need" was in fact a defense mechanism keeping men at a distance so she wouldn't be vulnerable. If no one was ever exquisite enough, she couldn't get hurt. What a big price to pay! By realized she was keeping everyone away, she was able to see the exquisiteness in all human beings and choose someone who would be ideal for her.

What about the woman who was in a panic that at age thirty she wasn't married? She felt the pressure from her community that she was past her prime. As a result of the coaching and having a breakthrough, she uncovered the "truth" that she really hadn't *wanted* to get married at age twenty-two, and in reality she'd had a great time traveling, volunteering, and living life in her twenties. That was her truth, and knowing it set her free to move on and find the one because she was finally ready.

Anything other than the truth causes suffering for no reason. Don't live someone else's life—live your own. Some people think there is a prize for carrying around a high volume of guilt, but there isn't. I coached a divorced, thirty-three-year-old woman who harbored hatred and anger toward her ex-husband. She wondered why no one was sending her date suggestions or fix-ups; it was a mystery to her. When we worked together, she realized that the gift of her seven-year marriage was her five-year-old daughter who she adored. With that paradigm shift, she was able to choose to forgive her ex-husband, and by doing so, she got to be free. She chose love and forgiveness over suffering, and her world opened up in a way she never thought possible. She chose to *be the one* and is now married to her true partner.

Or the woman you read about who decided as a child that she was spoiled and "didn't deserve" love or money, so she lived a life of punishment and deprivation. She married men who cheated on her and she always struggled financially; she even put her ex-husband through law school and only experienced the hard times with him. As a child, she felt guilty about the blessings in her life, and she decided along the way that she didn't deserve them. Uncovering the flaw in her belief system and accepting that she was in fact deserving of boundless love allowed her to break the life-long patterns in her love life. She also chose to change her career to one that was fulfilling and financially rewarding.

Another client was a thirty-two-year old man who would only date stunningly gorgeous women and wondered why they would reject him after a few months. "I can't be myself" he would say. "If I get angry or show any form of human emotion or intimacy, they reject me." His breakthrough came when he realized in the coaching that he was being phony when dating, and thus he attracted phony, like-minded women. There was a gap the size of the Grand Canyon between what he said he wanted (love, understanding, and partnership) and the kind of person he was being when dating (superficial, phony, and suave). The disconnect came from his need to cover up the "I'm not okay" story he'd invented when he was a nerdy, eleven-year-old kid who didn't fit in. He too got to open his eyes and choose to *be the one* in his life, and as a result, his life opened up and he began dating loving, understanding, and emotionally connected women.

And of course, this attitude of choosing doesn't end at "I do." The goal of Meet to Marry is not just to get married and be happy initially, but to get married and enjoy a lifetime of partnership and love. Achieving short-lived happiness isn't the end game here: growing as an individual and as a couple is, and seeing each other as new every day with gratitude and appreciation will keep your marriage "juicy," fresh, and wonderful. And that is why you should never stop growing, learning, and leaving your comfort zone when dating or in your marriage.

Choose to have a conscious, enduring relationship. Reject the bankrupt thinking that it's up to someone else to make you happy. Even in your future marriage, choose to be The One.

The following are testimonials from people who "came clean," "got into reality," and uncovered their own truths.

Meet to Marry coaching helped me see that I really didn't know what I needed in a relationship. The coaching taught me to be true to myself and to really see what had me blocked. I am now meeting women who are truly matched to my life vision.

—David, New York, NY

Bari's personal story is so inspiring! In spite of wanting to meet *the one,* I had been dreading dating. The support, guidance, and positive energy of the coaching give me hope and actually make me look forward to dating! The sessions and exercises have opened my eyes to where I was holding back, what I was scared of, and why I kept making the wrong choices. I now can move forward with confidence and excitement, plus it's given me a formula and structure to the process so it's not so daunting. I look forward to making better choices and being in a happy, healthy, and loving relationship!

—Anne, West Hartford, CT

As a relatively conservative woman, my expectation was that the onus for my single state lay on the shoulders of Mr. Right for having failed to find me. But the Meet to Marry coaching helped me to see what blind spots I had—things that I'm doing consciously or subconsciously that ward off that seemingly elusive thing called love—and begin to address them. I've been challenged to seek feedback from those closest to me on everything from my disposition to my wardrobe choices, and it's been a fun process of fine-tuning and enhancing who I am.

—Evelyn, Arlington, VA

Meet to Marry coaching is great! As hesitant as I was, I heard great things from a friend. The program opened my eyes to my patterns of neediness and control—choosing women who had enough love for both us. With the new information and the knowledge of how to overcome that lonely state of affairs, I made the adjustments necessary to attract a woman with whom I share a deep emotional commitment—and it's wonderful. We plan to be married in the spring.

—Joseph, Seattle, WA

Make the choice to bridge the gap between who are you are being and what you want. At the end of the day, there's only really one thing to do: Just be you—amazing, human, authentic, loveable YOU! *Be the One*!

Special Section for
Our Readers

I hope you enjoyed reading this book, and that it's left you with a new world of possibility for yourself and a new realm as it relates to dating and finding true love. My vision and mission is to transform how *all* people view dating and marriage. By taking on "being the one," anyone can have access to giving and receiving the unconditional love that we all need as human beings.

I also hope my story and the stories of others you've read about will inspire you to pursue the journey of "being the one"; this journey led me to a life I never thought possible. In the past, I used to wish away the time, and in my transformed world I savor the moments. I wish you every success and look forward to hearing your success stories.

Since personal growth is an evolution and a process of peeling away the layers, I'd like to share the ongoing resources available to you at the Meet to Marry site. You can use and experience all of the coaching materials you've read about. You can also take advantage of coaching programs, participate in webinars, special events, and find additional stories more at www.Meet ToMarry.com. In addition, I'd like to thank our valued readers by offering a discount for Meet to Marry services online. Visit www.MeetToMarry.com and use the promotional code BOOKPROMO for special offers and savings.

Acknowledgments

I am probably the most unlikely person to write a book about relationships, as people who knew me "before" would agree. As an eternal optimist, I wanted to share a different message: you can have it all, and you deserve to have it all, regardless of your circumstances. By choosing to see things differently, boundless love is available to everyone. There are many wonderful people to thank whose support made this project possible.

To Suzanne Falter-Barns of Get Known Now for helping me find my platform and my voice. To Barbara and David Messer for your support, generosity, and faith in us; you supported us in too many ways to mention and we're grateful. Chana Spivack, Richelle Doliner, Dina and Avraham Hendel, Rivkah Sidorsky, Yehudis Rumbak, Debra Chapman, and Anne LeBaron for your support and friendship. To Naomi Matatov, my appreciation for your dedication, enthusiasm, and commitment all those years. And to Margo Glover, my amazingly creative intern. Sol Kandel for your enthusiasm and passion about Meet to Marry from the moment you heard about the project. Imal Wagner, my literary agent and PR agent, for your enthusiasm, patience, and commitment to real love in the world and the adrenaline rush you create every time you call me.

Thank you to Eli Levy, Ph.D., for your enthusiasm and support about spreading the word that to find *the one*, you need to *be* the one, and for the support and for the wisdom you imparted to me on my own journey. You were truly one of my angels.

A big thank you to Thea Somers of Beyond Ten, whose ability "to get into my world" helped to propel me into my new reality. And to Hedy and Yumi Schleifer (http://www.hedyyumi.com/) for your love for people and commitment to a relationally mature world.

William (Willy) Mathes, my editor from Book Editor Coach, thanks for your enthusiasm and positive input. Namaste to you. Irene Hodes for her editing assistance and Jerrin Zumberg for her beautiful graphic design. And to countless singles whose privacy I will leave intact who shared their stories, who went through the coaching and pushed their own envelopes to connect to themselves and reach a new level of love and connection.

I've adopted family along the way, literally "adopted," and not an hour goes by that I'm not surrounded by one of our family members of rescued pets who provide the kind of gratitude and unconditional love we all look for in a relationship. Especially Sammy.

Finally, to my husband, Michael, for being a dream husband and champion and supporter of all possibilities for our lives. It truly was worth waiting a lifetime to find you. In you, I have found my soul mate and partner, the other half of myself who I'd been searching for forever. With you, there are no limits and I am profoundly grateful.

Recommended Reading and Resources

Al-Anon. *The 12 Steps of Alcoholics Anonymous.*

Beattie, Melody. *Codependent No More.* Hazelden Publishing, 2001.

Covey, Stephen R. *The 7 Habits of Highly Effective People.* Free Press, 2004.

Friedman, Manis. *Doesn't Anyone Blush Anymore?* Merkos Linyonei Chinuch, 1996.

Gibran, Kahlil. *The Prophet.* Knopf, 1995.

Godin, Seth. *Linchpin.* Porfolio Hardcover, 2010.

Goleman, Daniel. *Social Intelligence: The New Science of Human Relationships.* Bantam, 2007.

Hendrix, Harville. *Getting the Love You Want: A Guide for Couples.* Harry Holt, 2007.

———. *Keeping the Love You Find: A Personal Guide.* Atria, 1993.

Jungreis, Esther. *The Committed Marriage: A Guide to Finding a Soul Mate and Building a Relationship Through Timeless Biblical Wisdom.* Mesorah Publications Ltd., 2006.

———. *The Committed Life: Principles of Good Living from Our Timeless Past.* HarperOne, 1999.

"Landmark Education/The Forum" (www.landmarkeducation.com).

Saint-Exupéry, Antoine de. *The Little Prince*. Harcourt Brace, 1971.

Siegel, Daniel. *The Neurology of We*. Sounds True, Inc., 2008.

Whitfield, Charles L., M.D. *Healing the Child Within: Discovery and Recovery for Adult Children of Dysfunctional Families*. Health Communications, Inc., 1987.

Index